YOUR EVERY DAY INSTANT POT RECIPES:

TOP 120 AMAZING, HEALTHY, USEFUL, TASTED,

SIMPLE RECIPES FROM YOUR HOME ASISTANT

JOHN RANEY

Your Free Gift

I wanted to show my appreciation that you support my work so I've put together a free gift for you.

Get Your Free Gift Here:
http://www.ebookreadzone.com

Just visit the link above to download it now.

I know you will love this gift.

Thanks!

John Raney

Contents

Chapter 01: An introduction to instant pot

History

Pressure cooking is a strategy for cooking in a fixed vessel while at the same time, not allowing the steam to escape below a preset pressure. Since the breaking point of water increments as the pressure gets expanded, the pressure developed inside the cooker permits the fluid in the cooking pot to incline to a higher temperature before it gets boiled.

The instant pot was first manufactured by Denis Papin, who was a French physicist, in the year of 1679. But, it just turned into a family cooking machine during the Second World War Pressure cooking is regularly used to reenact the impacts of long braising or stewing in the shorter timeframes.

The Electric Instant pot

Routine instant pots were made to be utilized on the top of the stove. A steam controller, wellbeing valve, and pressure-actuated interlock instrument give security against overheating and the peril of blast. At the point when a pre-set pressure is come to in the cooker, the steam controller is pushed up by the pressure which is residing inside to permit the steam to get away.

An Electric instant pot comprises of a pressure cooking compartment, the electric warming component, and temperature or pressure sensors. The procedure of warming is controlled by the implicit scale processor in light of the readings of the pressure and temperature sensors. The guideline is like that of journey control found in numerous types of vehicles nowadays.

What do you have to know before buying Instant pot?

There is a wide range of offers on the web and some retail stores offering an extensive variety of offers and value ranges for instant pots. It will be ideal if you perform due steadiness when looking for your Instant Pot as you should not waste your money at any cost.

In case somebody offers you 18/10 stainless steel internal pot for lower than Instant Pot's value, you ought to request a declaration or evidence of the steel. There are likewise so many electric instant pots which use grade 202, which is another less expensive type of stainless steel.

Instant Pot's cooking pot is first made with a sheet of 18/8 grade of food. At that point, an aluminum plate and a spread circle of stainless steel base are melded on. The aluminum plate is not presented to food. The melding procedure abandons some fastening marks at within the cooking pot.
These patching imprints are cleaned away to make a cleaned internal surface, making the cooking pot less sticky for the food and simpler to clean.

Using and cleaning your instant pot

Here's the way to clean your Instant Pot, while taking into consideration the silicone ring that tends to clutch the smell of your scraps to continue everything in working request.

Fundamental post-supper cleanup

You can do it by washing the inward pot, and wiping down the lodging unit is the heft of keeping up a perfect machine. But, if capacities start to come up short, and you think you aren't getting the best possible seal during weight cooking.

Evacuating the silicone ring is a decent thing, to begin with. Since this piece should be all around situated for an appropriate seal, it ought to dependably be spotless and free of buildup before use. Also, when you set it back, check to ensure that it's fitted to the top safely, as well.

There are a couple of different parts that may bring about some kind of inconvenience for you. In case you make use of the quick release frequently, you may need to unscrew the counter piece shield for cleaning.

How to use it?

Use the Manual button

On the instant pot, the "Manual" button implies manual weight cooking, and the default temperature is high. Manual signifies physically planned weight cooking, rather than utilizing a system mode for programmed weight cooking.

Keep Warm mode does not influence the natural release of pressure. You should choose warming mode to accelerate characteristic weight discharge. It doesn't walk out
on until it achieves the heating scope of 145°F to 172°F, which is well below the temperature where the weight will discharge.

Different modes in Instant pot to work with

Keep Warm/Cancel

This is the most vital key since when Instant Pot is being customized or any system that is used as a basic. By selecting this "Keep Warm/Cancel," Instant Pot Pressure Cooker will wipe out the project and take the cooker to standby rate.

Meat/Stew

This mode is basically used for cooking meat and stew.
Once more, the key of "Adjust" can be utilized to change the cooking time to get the accomplished surface of the meat.

Rice

This mode is a completely mechanized brilliant system for cooking normal rice or parboiled rice. The cooking span is balanced consequently relying upon the measure of food you are going to make.

Poultry

This mode is being modified in making poultry dishes. You may utilize the "Alter" key to change the poultry cooking time from "Typical" to "Additional" or "Less" contingent upon your inclination of the composition and the measure of poultry you put into the pot.

Soup

This key is for making soups and stock.
In case you need to have a hot soup when you are sitting tight on your breakfast, you can utilize the "select key" to choose for a cooking span.

Steam

This is intended for steaming vegetables, fish with the encased steam rack. While steaming vegetables and fish, don't utilize the "Quick release" mode for discharging the steam since it will probably overcook the sustenance

. Bean/Chili

This is the mode which is used for cooking beans and making stew. Presently in case you need the beans to be completely cooked, make use of the "Adjust" key to expand the time.Porridge

This mode is for making porridge of different grains. You can utilize the key of "Adjust" to choose the time for cooking. The "Normal" span is for rice porridge. For a blend of various grains and beans, you pick the "More" key.

Chapter 02: Delicious Recipes for Babies (6 months – 12 months)

Recipe 1: Tasty rice cereal

Servings: 02
Cooking Time: 20 Minutes
Complexity Level: Easy
Vegetarian/Non-vegetarian: Vegetarian
Mode: Porridge/soup/rice

Ingredients:

- Uncooked rice powder 1 cup
- Water: 2 quarter cups
- Maple syrup: 2 tablespoons
- One pinch salt

Directions:

Add water, maple syrup and rice powder to the instant pot.

Cover its lid and select "Porridge" and cook on the manual setting. Once you get the sound of the beep, turn the instant pot off and wait for ten to fifteen minutes. Now, select the option of "Quick Release" to release any kind of pressure that resides inside.

After that, carefully attempt to remove the lid and wait for the steam to completely get dispersed. Now, take the cooked cereal out and serve it warm.

Advice:If you like then you can replace rice powder with normal rice as well

Nutrion Value:

- **Servings Size: Half cup**
- **Calories: 2987**
- **Sodium: 132.2mg,**
- **Total Fat: 122g,**
- **Carbohydrates: 63.211g,**
- **Protein: 12g**

Recipe 2: Instant Pot chicken broth

- **Serving:** 5
- **Cooking Time:** 25 Minutes
- **Cooking Level:** Easy
- **Vegetarian/Non-vegetarian:** Non-vegetarian
- **Mode:** Porridge/Poultry/Multigrain

Ingredients:

- **Boneless chicken (breast): Half pound**
- **Salt: Half teaspoon**
- **Black pepper: as you require**
- **Water: 1 cup**

Directions:

Season the chicken with salt and pepper and coat all the pieces of chicken very well. Put the coated chicken in an instant pot and add water to it. Carefully cover with its lid and press "Poultry" button.

Once you get to hear the beep from the instant pot, carefully release pressure with the help of instant release. Take out the chicken broth by keeping Strainer in a bowl and serve warm.

Advice: Chicken with bones will also work well, but it's a bit time consuming.

Nutritional Information:

- **Servings Size**: Half cup
- **Calories:** 20
- **Fiber:** 1g,
- **Protein**: 20g,
- **Carb:** 3g,
- **Fat:** 3 g,
- **Sugar:** 0g,
- **Cholesterol:** 2 mg,
- **Sodium:** 360 mg

Recipe 3: Instant pot Oatmeal porridge

- **Servings:** 2
- **Cooking Time:** 25 Minutes
- **Vegetarian/Non-vegetarian:** Vegetarian
- **Mode:** Porridge/Multigrain

Ingredients:

- Salt: 1 teaspoon
- Black pepper: 1/8 teaspoon
- Olive oil: 1 teaspoon
- Ground oats: 1 cup
- Water: 1 cup

Directions:

Set your instant pot to "Porridge" and once it turns "hot" you are required to add oats, black pepper, olive oil, salt and water in it.

Then cover its lid and cook the mixture on "Porridge" for 2 minutes. After hearing the final beep sound, release pressure via quick release and take out the porridge. Transfer it to the bowl and serve warm.

Advice: If desirable, you can replace the olive oil with sunflower oil as well.

Nutritional Information:

- **Serving Size:** 1 Cup
- **Calories:** 212
- **Fiber:** 0 g
- **Total Fat:** 5 g
- **Sodium:** 732mg
- **Cholesterol:** 21mg
- **Saturated Fat:**1g
- **Protein:** 20g and Sugar- 2g

Recipe 4: Instant pot apricots

- **Servings:** 2
- **Cooking Time:** 20 Minutes
- **Complexity Level:** Easy
- **Vegetarian/Non-vegetarian:** Vegetarian
- **Mode:** Steam

Ingredients:

- **Dried apricots: 1 pound**
- **Water: 2 cups**
- **White grapes juice or apple juice: 1 cup**

Directions:

Add water, dried apricots and apple or grapes juice to the instant pot. Cover its lid and select "Steam" and cook on the automatic setting. Once you get beep sound, turn the instant pot off and wait for fifteen minutes.

Carefully remove the lid and wait for the steam to completely disperse. Take it out of the instant pot and serve warm or if you want, then you can serve it after getting it cool as well. But do not serve chilled.

Advice: Instead of Apple juice, you can use pineapple syrup as well.

Nutritional Value:

- **Servings Size:** Half cup
- **Calories:** 2987
- **Sodium:** 132.2mg
- **Total Fat:** 122g,
- **Carbohydrates:** 63.211g
- **Protein**: 12g

Recipe 5: Instant Pot apple puree

- **Serving:** 5
- **Cooking Time:** 25 Minutes
- **Cooking Level:** Easy
- **Vegetarian/Non-vegetarian:** Vegetarian
- **Mode:** Steam

Ingredients:

- **Apples (peeled):** 2
- **Sugar:** as per taste
- **Cumin:** ¾ teaspoon
- **Water:** 1 cup

Directions:

Take apples, sugar, cumin, and water in an instant pot so that the apples get dipped in water. Carefully cover with its lid and press "Steam" button.

Once you hear the final beep of instant pot, carefully release pressure with the help of instant release. Take out the mixture and add it to the serving bowl.

Advice: Cumin will add an extra flavor, but if desirable, you can skip adding it to the recipe.

Nutritional Information:

- **Servings Size:** Half cup
- **Calories:** 20
- **Fiber:** 1g
- **Protein:** 20g
- **Carb:** 3g
- **Fat:** 3 g
- **Sugar:** 0g
- **Cholesterol:** 2 mg
- **Sodium:** 360 mg

Recipe 6: Chicken and potato salsa

- **Servings:** 2
- **Cooking Time:** 25 Minutes
- **Vegetarian/Non-vegetarian:** Non-vegetarian
- **Mode:** Porridge/Soup

Ingredients:

- **Chicken boneless: 1 pound**
- **Salt: 1 teaspoon**
- **Black pepper: 1/8 teaspoon**
- **Olive oil: 1 teaspoon**
- **Potato: 1**

Directions:

Put boneless chicken, salt, black pepper, olive oil and potato in the instant pot and set your instant pot to "Saute" and once it turns "hot", you have to add oil. You have to cook chicken and potato for almost 20 minutes.

Once you hear the final beep sound, release pressure via quick release and take out the chicken and potato and its sauces from the instant pot. Blend the mixture so that potato and chicken become consistent. Put the along sauce in a bowl and garnish with black pepper. Serve warm.

Advice: *Replace olive oil with sunflower oil to give it a better taste, if you do not like olive oil.*

Nutritional Information:

- **Serving Size:** 1 Cup
- **Calories:** 212
- **Fiber:** 0 g
- **Total Fat:** 5 g
- **Sodium:** 732mg
- **Cholesterol:** 21mg
- **Saturated Fat:** 1g
- **Protein:** 20g
- **Sugar:** 2g

Recipe 7: Instant pot mashed avocado

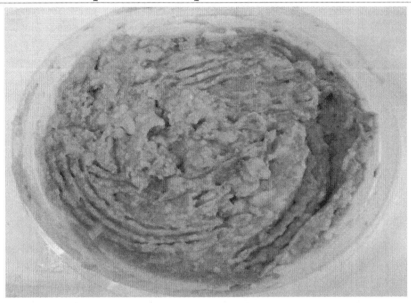

- **Servings:** 2
- **Cooking Time:** 20 Minutes
- **Complexity Level:** Easy
- **Vegetarian/Non-vegetarian:** Vegetarian
- **Mode:** Porridge/Steam

Ingredients:

- **Avocado (peeled): 2**
- **Sugar: as per taste**
- **Cumin: ¾ teaspoon**
- **Water: 1 cup**

Directions:

Take avocado, sugar, cumin and water in an instant pot so that the avocado get dipped in water. Carefully cover with its lid and press "Steam" button.

Once you hear the final beep of instant pot, carefully release pressure with the help of instant release. Take out the mixture and add it to the serving bowl. You can also serve it after blending in the blender.

Advice: If desirable, replace water with pineapple syrup to give it even better taste.

Nutritional Value:

- **Servings Size:** Half cup
- **Calories:** 2987
- **Sodium:** 132.2mg
- **Total Fat:** 122g
- **Carbohydrates:** 63.211g
- **Protein:** 12g

Recipe 8: Banana and apples mush

- **Serving:** 5
- **Cooking Time:** 25 Minutes
- **Cooking Level:** Easy
- **Vegetarian/Non-vegetarian:** Vegetarian
- **Mode:** Steam/Multigrain

Ingredients:

- **Bananas: 2**
- **Salt: A pinch**
- **Apple (peeled): 1**
- **Sugar: 2 tablespoon**
- **Water: Half cup**

Directions:

Put bananas, water, salt, apple and sugar in an instant pot and carefully cover with its lid and press "steam" button.

Once you hear the final beep of instant pot, carefully release pressure with the help of the option of "instant release". Take out cooked mixture and keep it in a bowl. Serve warm.

Advice: You can add apples without peeling them off, it will give a chunky texture to the recipe.

Nutritional Information:

- **Servings Size:** Half cup
- **Calories:** 20
- **Fiber:** 1g
- **Protein:** 20g
- **Carb:** 3g
- **Fat:** 3 g
- **Sugar:** 0g
- **Cholesterol:** 2 mg
- **Sodium:** 360 mg

Recipe 9: Instant pot mashed mangoes and banana

- Servings: 2
- Cooking Time: 25 Minutes
- Vegetarian/Non-vegetarian: Vegetarian
- Mode: Porridge/Steam

Ingredients:

- Bananas: 2
- Sugar: 1 tablespoon
- Olive oil: 1 teaspoon
- Mangoes (peeled): 2

Directions:

Add mangoes, sugar, olive oil and bananas in the instant pot. Mix them well and leave for a few hours (if you have time; otherwise, start cooking). Set your instant pot to "Steam".

Cover its lid and cook the fruits for 2 minutes. Once you hear the final beep sound, release pressure via quick release and take out the mixture and mash them up. Serve it in a bowl.

Advice: Replace olive oil with cooking oil to give a different taste.

Nutritional Information:

- **Serving Size: 1 Cup**
- **Calories: 212**
- **Fiber: 0 g**
- **Total Fat: 5 g**
- **Sodium: 732mg**
- **Cholesterol: 21mg**
- **Saturated Fat: 1g**
- **Protein: 20g**
- **Sugar: 2g**

Recipe 10: Instant pot sweet carrots

- Servings: 2
- Cooking Time: 20 Minutes
- Complexity Level: Easy
- Vegetarian/Non-vegetarian: Vegetarian
- Mode: Steam

Ingredients:

- Peeled carrots: 2
- Water: 2 quarter cups
- Maple syrup: 2 tablespoons
- Vanilla: Half teaspoon
- One pinch salt

Directions:

Add peeled carrots, water, maple syrup, vanilla and a pinch of salt to the instant pot.

Cover its lid and select "steam" and cook on the manual setting. Once you get beep sound, turn the instant pot off and wait for ten minutes. Carefully remove the lid and wait for the steam to completely disperse.

Advice: If desirable, replace maple syrup with pineapple syrup to give it even better taste.

Nutritional Value:

- **Servings Size: Half cup**
- **Calories: 2987**
- **Sodium: 132.2mg**
- **Total Fat: 122g**
- **Carbohydrates: 63.211g**
- **Protein:12g**

Chapter 03: Delicious Recipes for Toddlers

Recipe 1: Quinoa for Breakfast

- Servings: 06
- Cooking Time: 15 Minutes
- Complexity Level: Easy
- Vegetarian/Non-vegetarian: Vegetarian
- Mode: Porridge

Ingredients:

- Uncooked Quinoa (rinse it well): 1 ½ cup
- Water: 2 ¼ cups
- Maple syrup: 2 tablespoons
- Vanilla: ½ teaspoon
- Ground cinnamon: ¼ teaspoon
- One pinch salt

Toppings:

- Fresh Berries
- Chopped Almonds
- Milk

Directions:

Add water, vanilla, maple syrup, cinnamon, salt, and quinoa to the instant pot.

Cover its lid and select "Porridge" and cook on the manual setting. Once you get beep sound, turn the instant pot off and wait for ten minutes. Now, use "Quick Release" to release any pressure.

Carefully remove the lid and wait for the steam to completely disperse. It is time to fluff the quinoa and serve with berries, almonds, and milk.

Advice: If desirable, replace maple syrup with pineapple syrup to give it even better taste.

Nutritional Value:

- Calories: 361.25
- Sodium: 149.61mg
- Total Fat: 13.14g
- Carbohydrates: 53.62g
- Protein: 11.75g

Recipe 2: Instant Pot Shredded Chicken Salsa

- Serving: 5
- Cooking Time: 30 Minutes
- Cooking Level: Easy
- Vegetarian/Non-vegetarian: Non-vegetarian
- Mode: Porridge/Poultry

Ingredients:

- Boneless chicken (breast): 1 pound
- Kosher salt: ½ teaspoon
- Black pepper: as per taste
- Cumin: ¾ teaspoon
- Oregano: 1 pinch
- Chunky salsa: 1 cup

Directions:

Season all spices on chicken and coat these pieces well. Put chicken in a greased instant pot and pour salsa over chicken pieces. Carefully cover with its lid and press "Poultry" button. Make sure to increase 5 minutes in default cooking time to cook chicken for almost 20 minutes.

Once you hear the final beep of instant pot, carefully release pressure with the help of instant release. Take out chicken with a tong and keep it on a plate. Shred all chicken pieces completely with the help of two forks.

Pour leftover juices of chicken in the instant pot on shredded chicken and serve with boiled rice or brown bread.

Advice: If desirable, replace chunky salsa with fruit cocktail to give it even better taste.

Nutritional Information:

- **Servings Size: ½ cup**
- **Calories: 125**
- **Fiber: 1g**
- **Protein: 22g**
- **Carb: 3g**
- **Fat: 3 g**
- **Sugar: 0g**
- **Cholesterol: 6 mg**
- **Sodium: 379 mg**

Recipe 3: Drumsticks with Tomato Sauce

- Servings: 6
- Cooking Time: 30 Minutes
- Vegetarian/Non-vegetarian: Non-vegetarian
- Mode: Porridge/sauté

Ingredients:

- Chicken Drumsticks: 6
- Cider vinegar: 1 tablespoon
- Kosher salt: 1 teaspoon
- **Black pepper: 1/8 teaspoon**
- **Dried oregano: 1 teaspoon**
- **Olive oil: 1 teaspoon**
- **Tomato sauce: 1 ½ cups**
- **Chopped cilantro: ¼ cup**
- **Jalapeno (remove seeds and halved): 1**

Directions:

Season all chicken pieces with pepper, salt, vinegar, and oregano. Mix them well and leave for a few hours (if you have time; otherwise, start cooking).

Set your instant pot to "Saute" and once it turns "hot" you have to add oil. You have to cook chicken for almost 8 minutes (4 minutes for each side) to let it brown.

It is time to add tomato sauce, cilantro (2 tablespoons) and jalapeno.

Cover its lid and cook chicken on "Poultry" for 20 minutes. Once you hear the final beep sound, release pressure via quick release and take out the chicken and its sauces from the instant pot. Put chicken along sauce in a bowl and garnish with cilantro. Serve these drumsticks with white rice.

Advice: If desirable, replace dried oregano with dried mint leaves to give it even better taste.

Nutritional Information:

- **Serving Size: 1 Drumstick**
- **Calories:161**
- **Fiber: 0 g**
- **Total Fat: 5 g**
- **Sodium: 736mg**
- **Cholesterol:101mg**
- **Saturated Fat: 1g**
- **Protein: 22g**
- **Sugar: 2g**

Recipe 4: Instant Pot vegetable combo

- Serving: 2
- Cooking Time: 25 Minutes
- Cooking Level: Easy
- Vegetarian/Non-vegetarian: Vegetarian
- Mode: Steam

Ingredients:

- Green Beans: Quarter cup
- Summer Squash: Half cup
- Peas: Half cup
- Carrots: Quarter cup
- Water: 2 cups

Directions:

Add green beans, summer squash, peas, carrots and water to the instant pot and set it to "steam". Make sure to increase 2 minutes in default cooking time to cook peas for almost 20 minutes.

Once you hear the final beep of instant pot, carefully release pressure with the help of instant release. Take out the mixture with a spatula and place it in bowl. Pour leftover juices of vegetables in the instant pot on the cooked vegetables and serve warm.

Advice: If desirable, you can add some more vegetables as well.

Nutritional Information:

- **Servings Size: Half cup**
- **Calories: 20**
- **Fiber: 1g**
- **Protein: 20g**
- **Carb: 3g**
- **Fat: 3 g**
- **Sugar: 0g**
- **Cholesterol: 2 mg**
- **Sodium: 360 mg**

Recipe 5: Instant pot sweet tomatoes

- Servings: 2
- Cooking Time: 25 Minutes
- Vegetarian/Non-vegetarian: Vegetarian
- Mode: Yoghurt

Ingredients:

- Peeled tomatoes: 2
- Water: 2 cups
- Vanilla: Half teaspoon
- One pinch salt
- Sugar: 4 tablespoon

Directions:

Add peeled tomatoes, water, vanilla, sugar and a pinch of salt to the instant pot. Cover its lid and select "steam" and cook on the manual setting. Once you get beep sound, turn the instant pot off and wait for ten minutes. Now, use "Quick Release" so that the remaining pressure can be released. Carefully remove the lid and wait for the steam so that it gets completely dispersed.

Advice: You can skip vanilla if desirable, it will give a better taste to your recipe.

Nutritional Information:

- **Serving Size: 1 Cup**
- **Calories: 212**
- **Fiber: 0 g**
- **Total Fat: 5 g**
- **Sodium: 732mg**
- **Cholesterol: 21mg**
- **Saturated Fat: 1g**
- **Protein: 20g**
- **Sugar: 2g**

Recipe 6: Instant pot chicken with sweet potatoes

- Servings: 2
- Cooking Time: 20 Minutes
- Complexity Level: Easy
- Vegetarian/Non-vegetarian: Non-Vegetarian
- Mode: Steam/Multigrain

Ingredients:

- Uncooked sweet potatoes: 2
- Water: 2 quarter cups
- Vanilla: Half teaspoon
- Ground cinnamon: quarter teaspoon
- One pinch salt
- Sugar: 2 tablespoon
- Chicken (boneless): 1 pound

Directions:

Add water, vanilla, sweet potatoes, cinnamon, salt, and chicken to the instant pot. Cover its lid and select "Porridge" and cook on the manual setting. Once you get beep sound, turn the instant pot off and wait for ten minutes. Now, use "Quick Release" option to release any pressure.

Carefully remove the lid and wait for the steam to completely disperse. It is time to fluff the quinoa and serve with berries, almonds, and milk.

Advice: *You better use fresh sweet potatoes to avoid any lumps after mashing them.*

Nutritional Value:

- **Servings Size: 1 cup**
- **Calories: 2987**
- **Sodium: 132.2mg**
- **Total Fat: 122g**
- **Carbohydrates: 63.211g,**
- **Protein: 12g**

Recipe 7: Instant Pot Shredded Chicken with avocado

- Serving: 5
- Cooking Time: 25 Minutes
- Cooking Level: Easy
- Vegetarian/Non-vegetarian: Non-vegetarian
- Mode: Porridge/Poultry/Steam

Ingredients:

- Boneless chicken (breast): 2 pound
- Salt: Quarter teaspoon
- Black pepper: as per taste
- Cumin: ¾ teaspoon
- Oregano: 1 pinch
- Avocado (peeled): 2

Directions:

Season the chicken with salt, black pepper, cumin and oregano and coat these pieces well. Put chicken along with avocado in a greased instant pot and pour salsa over chicken pieces.

Carefully cover with its lid and press "Poultry" button. Make sure to increase 5 minutes in default cooking time to cook chicken for almost 20 minutes. Once you hear the final beep of instant pot, carefully release pressure with the help of instant release. Serve.

Advice: Replace cumin with coriander if desired.

Nutritional Information:

- **Servings Size: Half cup**
- **Calories: 20**
- **Fiber: 1g**
- **Protein: 20g**
- **Carb: 3g**
- **Fat: 3 g**
- **Sugar: 0g**
- **Cholesterol: 2 mg**
- **Sodium: 360 mg**

Recipe 8: Instant pot chicken and vegetable salsa

- Servings: 2
- Cooking Time: 25 Minutes
- Vegetarian/Non-vegetarian: Non-vegetarian
- Mode: Porridge/Poultry

Ingredients:

- Chicken (boneless): 2 pounds
- Cider vinegar: 2 tablespoon
- Kosher salt: Half teaspoon
- Black pepper: 1/4 teaspoon
- Dried oregano: 1 teaspoon
- Olive oil: 1 teaspoon
- Tomato sauce: 1 cups
- Chopped cilantro: quarter cup
- Jalapeno (remove seeds and halved): 1
- Cooked canned vegetables: Half can

Directions:

Season all chicken pieces with pepper, salt, vinegar, and oregano. Mix them well and leave for an hour. Set your instant pot to "Sauté" and then you have to add oil. You have to cook chicken for almost 20 minutes to let it brown.

It is time to add tomato sauce, cilantro and jalapeno. Add the canned vegetables as well. Cover its lid and cook chicken on "Poultry" for twenty minutes. Once you hear the final beep sound, release pressure via quick release and take out the chicken and its sauces from the instant pot.

Put chicken along sauce in a bowl and garnish with cilantro. Serve in a bowl.

Advice: If desirable, replace kosher salt with normal sea salt.

Nutritional Information:

- Serving Size: 1 Cup
- Calories: 212
- Fiber: 0 g
- Total Fat: 5 g
- Sodium: 732mg
- Cholesterol: 21mg
- Saturated Fat: 1g
- Protein: 20g
- Sugar: 2g

Recipe 9: Mashed potatoes with Tomato Sauce

- Servings: 1
- Cooking Time: 20 Minutes
- Complexity Level: Easy
- Vegetarian/Non-vegetarian: Vegetarian
- Mode: Porridge/Multigrain

Ingredients:

- Uncooked potatoes: 1 cup
- Water: 2 quarter cups
- Maple syrup: 2 tablespoons
- Vanilla: Half teaspoon
- Tomatoes: 2 (medium sized)
- A pinch of salt

Directions:

Add water, vanilla, maple syrup, cinnamon, salt, and quinoa to the instant pot. Then add tomatoes in it as well.

Cover its lid and select "Porridge" and cook on the manual setting. Once you get beep sound, turn the instant pot off and wait for ten minutes. Now, use "Quick Release" to release any pressure.

Now remove the lid of the instant pot and wait for the steam to completely disperse. It is time to fluff the quinoa and serve with berries, almonds, and milk.

Advice: Do not add tomatoes until you peel them. The tomato skin will not come out with a good taste.

Nutritional Value:

- **Calories: 2987,**
- **Sodium: 132.2mg,**
- **Total Fat: 122g,**
- **Carbohydrates: 63.211g,**
- **Protein: 12g**

Recipe 10: Instant Pot mixed fruits

- Serving: 5
- Cooking Time: 25 Minutes
- Cooking Level: Easy
- Vegetarian/Non-vegetarian: Vegetarian
- Mode: Steam

Ingredients:

- Avocado: 1 pound
- Sugar: Half teaspoon
- Black pepper: as per taste
- Cumin: 2 teaspoon
- Mango: 2 (peeled)
- Chunky fruit cocktail: 1 cup
- Water: 1 cup

Directions:

Add avocado, sugar, cumin, black pepper, mango and chunky fruit cocktail in the instant pot. Carefully cover with its lid and press "steam" button. Once you hear the final beep of instant pot, carefully release pressure with the help of instant release. Take out the mixture and pour it into the bowl.

Advice: If desirable, replace water with cocktail syrup to give it even better taste.

Nutritional Information:

- **Servings Size: Half cup**
- **Calories: 20**
- **Fiber: 1g**
- **Protein: 20g**
- **Carb: 3g**
- **Fat: 3 g**
- **Sugar: 2g**
- **Cholesterol: 2 mg**
- **Sodium: 360 mg**

Chapter 04: Instant pot breakfast recipes

Recipe 1: Low-Fat instant pot breakfast

-
- Cooking Time: 45 Minutes
- Cooking Level: Easy
- Vegetarian/Non-vegetarian: Non-Vegetarian
- Mode: Steam

Ingredients:

- Apples which are peeled: Half kg
- Cinnamon: 1 teaspoon
- Cardamom: 1 teaspoon
- Ginger: 1 teaspoon
- Lemon: 1 medium sized

Methods:

Add all the above ingredients to your instant pot and stir all well with the help of a wooden spoon. You may cook the above mixture for about 45 minutes on your instant pot. Carefully cover with its lid and press "porridge" button. Once you hear the final beep of instant pot, carefully release pressure with the help of instant release. Take out the mixture and pour it into the bowl.

Advice: *If you want, replace water with stock to give it even better taste.*

Nutritional Information:

- **Servings Size: 2 cup**
- **Calories: 45**
- **Fiber: 1g**
- **Protein: 45g**
- **Carb: 3g**
- **Fat: 0.2 g**
- **Sugar: 2g**
- **Cholesterol: 0.3 mg**
- **Sodium: 360 mg**

Recipe 2: Instant pot Tomato soup

- Cooking Time: 25 Minutes
- Cooking Level: Easy
- Vegetarian/Non-vegetarian: Vegetarian
- Mode: Steam

Ingredients:

- Tomatoes: 1
- Yellow onions: 1
- Garlic cloves: 5
- Parsley: 1 tbsp.
- Tomatoes paste: 2 tbsp.
- Salt and pepper: As required

Method:

Put all the ingredients in an instant pot. Carefully cover with its lid and press "steam" button. Once you hear the final beep of instant pot, carefully release pressure with the help of instant release. Take out the mixture and pour it into the bowl.

Advice: If you want, replace water with chicken stock to give it even better taste.

Nutritional Information:

- **Servings Size: 2 cup**
- **Calories: 45**
- **Fiber: 1g**
- **Protein: 45g**
- **Carb: 3g**
- **Fat: 0.4 g**
- **Sugar: 2g**
- **Cholesterol: 0.1 mg**
- **Sodium: 360 mg**

Recipe 3: Low-Fat instant pot porridge

- Cooking Time: 45 Minutes
- Cooking Level: Easy
- Vegetarian/Non-vegetarian: Vegetarian
- Mode: Steam

Ingredients:

- Onion: 1
- Salt and black pepper: As per taste
- Potatoes: 1
- Tomatoes paste: 3 tablespoon
- Fresh thyme: 1 tbsp.
- Oats: 1 cup
- Toasted almonds: ½ cup

Method:

Take an instant pot, add onion and tomatoes in it. Take curry powder and add it to the mixture and pour this mixture into the instant pot. Add rest of the ingredients. Carefully cover with its lid and press "steam" button. Once you hear the final beep of instant pot, carefully release pressure with the help of instant release. Take out the mixture and pour it into the bowl.

Advice: *If you want, replace almonds with peanuts to give it even better taste.*

Nutritional Information:

- **Servings Size: 2 cup**
- **Calories: 45**
- **Fiber: 1g**
- **Protein: 45g**
- **Carb: 3g**
- **Fat: 0.5 mg**
- **Sugar: 2g**
- **Cholesterol: 0.5 mg**
- **Sodium: 360 mg**

Recipe 4: Low-Fat tortilla porridge recipe

- Cooking Time: 45 Minutes
- Cooking Level: Easy
- Vegetarian/Non-vegetarian: Vegetarian
- Mode: Steam

Ingredients:

- Tomatoes: 2
- Onion: 2
- Jalapenos: 1
- Carrots: 1 cups
- Cumin: 1 tbsp.
- Chili powder: 2 teaspoon
- Water: 1 cup

Method:

Take an instant pot, add ingredients, and then carefully cover with its lid and press "steam" button. Once you hear the final beep of instant pot, carefully release pressure with the help of instant release. Take out the mixture and pour it into the bowl.

Advice: If you want, replace water with stock to give it even better taste.

Nutritional Information:

- **Servings Size: 2 cup**
- **Calories: 45**
- **Fiber: 1g**
- **Protein: 45g**
- **Carb: 3g**
- **Fat: 0.3 g**
- **Sugar: 2g**
- **Cholesterol: 0 mg**
- **Sodium: 360 mg**

Recipe 5: Low-Fat French toast

- Cooking Time: 15 Minutes
- Cooking Level: Easy
- Vegetarian/Non-vegetarian: Vegetarian
- Mode: Steam

Ingredients:

- Bread: 2 slices
- Sugar: 2 tablespoon
- Egg whites: Two
- Oil: 1 tablespoon
- Milk: 1 kg

Method:

Take bread and cut its sides. Blend egg whites and add sugar in them. Dip the bread into the egg and then add to instant pot. Carefully cover with its lid and press "steam" button. You can also enter the manual option for about five minutes. Once you hear the final beep of instant pot, carefully release pressure with the help of instant release. Take out the mixture into the bowl.

Advice: If you want, you can add a pinch of vanilla essence in eggs as well, while beating.

Nutritional Information:

- **Servings Size: 2 cup**
- **Calories: 45**
- **Fiber: 1g**
- **Protein: 45g**
- **Carb: 3g**
- **Fat: 0.1 g**
- **Sugar: 2g**
- **Cholesterol: 0.2 mg**
- **Sodium: 360 mg**

Chapter 05: Instant pot lunch recipes

Recipe 1: Vinegar Low-Fat chicken steak

- Cooking Time: 20 Minutes
- Cooking Level: Easy
- Vegetarian/Non-vegetarian: Non-Vegetarian
- Mode: Steam

Ingredients:

- Boneless chicken 1 kg
- Soy sauce 1 tsp.
- Salt as per your taste
- Vinegar 1 tsp.

Method:

Combine all ingredients in a bowl. Transfer them to instant pot having hot oil. Add water and then carefully cover with its lid and press "steam" button. Once you hear the final beep of instant pot, carefully release pressure with the help of instant release

Advice: If you do not like, then you can definitely skip vinegar to make taste as per you like.

Nutritional Information:

- Servings Size: 3 cups
- Calories: 40
- Fiber: 1g
- Protein: 35
- Carb: 3g
- Fat: 0.5 g
- Sugar: 3g
- Cholesterol: 3 mg
- Sodium: 255 mg

Recipe 2: Low-Fat chicken steak dumplings

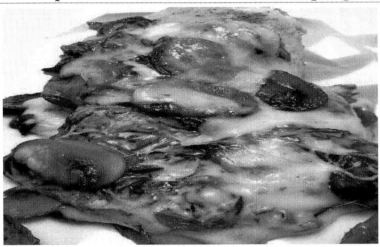

- Cooking Time: 20 Minutes
- Cooking Level: Easy
- Vegetarian/Non-vegetarian: Non-Vegetarian
- Mode: Steam

Ingredients:

- Minced chicken one cups
- Corn flour 1 tsp.
- Barbeque sauce 1 tsp.
- Eggs one beaten
- Salt as per your taste
- Black pepper 1 tsp.

Method:

Mix well all the ingredients in a bowl and leave for about one hour to get marinated. Cover its lid and select "Porridge" and cook on the manual setting. Once you get beep sound, turn the instant pot off and wait for ten minutes. Now, use "Quick Release" to release any pressure. Now remove the lid of the instant pot and wait for the steam to completely disperse. Dish out and serve with chili garlic sauce with whole-wheat bread.

Advice: If you want, replace barbeque sauce with soy sauce to give it even better taste.

Nutritional Information:

- Servings Size: 5 cups
- Calories: 40
- Fiber: 1g
- Protein: 35
- Carb: 3g
- Fat: 0.5 g
- Sugar: 3g
- Cholesterol: 3 mg
- Sodium: 255 mg

Recipe 3: Yummy white Chicken casserole

- Cooking Time: 35 Minutes
- Cooking Level: Easy
- Vegetarian/Non-vegetarian: Non-Vegetarian
- Mode: Poultry

Ingredients:

- Potatoes 1 boiled and mashed
- Chicken boneless one kg
- Vinegar 1 tsp.
- Soy sauce 1 tsp.
- Salt as per your taste
- Black pepper flakes 1 tsp.
- Milk one cups

Method:

Place all the ingredients in an instant pot. Add water and then carefully cover with its lid and press "steam" button. Once you hear the final beep of instant pot, carefully release pressure with the help of instant release

Advice: If you want, replace water with stock to give it even better taste.

Nutritional Information:

- Servings Size: 3 cups
- Calories: 40
- Fiber: 1g
- Protein: 35
- Carb: 3g
- Fat: 0.5 g
- Sugar: 3g
- Cholesterol: 3 mg
- Sodium: 255 mg

Recipe 4: Soy chicken

- **Cooking Time: 20 Minutes**
- **Cooking Level: Easy**
- **Vegetarian/Non-vegetarian: Non-Vegetarian**
- **Mode: Steam**

Ingredients:

- **Soy sauce one cups**
- **Chicken one kg**
- **Corn flour 1 tsp.**
- **Salt as per your taste**
- **Black pepper one tsp.**
- **Vinegar 1 tsp.**

Method:

Combine all ingredients in the instant pot. Cover its lid and select "Porridge" and cook on the manual setting. Once you get beep sound, turn the instant pot off and wait for ten minutes. Now, use "Quick

Release" to release any pressure. Now remove the lid of the instant pot and wait for the steam to completely disperse.

Advice: If you want, replace black pepper with white pepper to give it even better taste.

Nutritional Information:

- **Servings Size: 2 cups**
- **Calories: 40**
- **Fiber: 1g**
- **Protein: 35**
- **Carb: 3g**
- **Fat: 0.5 g**
- **Sugar: 3g**
- **Cholesterol: 3 mg**
- **Sodium: 255 mg**

Recipe 5: Simply delicious fried chicken

- Cooking Time: 35 Minutes
- Cooking Level: Easy
- Vegetarian/Non-vegetarian: Non-Vegetarian
- Mode: Steam

Ingredients:

- Oil 1 tsp.
- Chicken one kg
- Pepper and salt as per your taste
- Vinegar 1 tsp.
- Olives chopped 1 tsp.
- Oregano leaves 1 tsp.

Method:

Add chicken and all the other ingredients in an instant pot. Add water and then carefully cover with its lid and press "steam" button. Once you hear the final beep of instant pot, carefully release pressure with the help of instant release

Advice: If you want, replace water with stock to give it even better taste.

Nutritional Information:

- **Servings Size: 2 cups**
- **Calories: 40**
- **Fiber: 1g**
- **Protein: 35**
- **Carb: 3g**
- **Fat: 0.5 g**
- **Sugar: 3g**
- **Cholesterol: 3 mg**
- **Sodium: 255 mg**

Recipe 6: Spinach and onion chicken

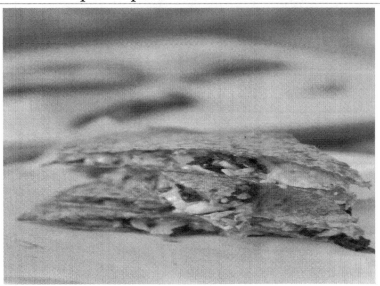

- Cooking Time: 25 Minutes
- Cooking Level: Easy
- Vegetarian/Non-vegetarian: Non-Vegetarian
- Mode: Poultry

Ingredients:

- Chicken one kg minced
- Spinach one cups boiled and mashed
- Oil 1 tsp.
- Salt to taste
- Black pepper 1 tsp.
- Onion chopped 1 cups

Method:

Combine all the ingredients in a bowl except oil. Take an instant pot and add the mix in it along with oil. Cover its lid and select "Porridge" and cook on the manual setting. Once you get beep sound, turn the instant pot off and wait for ten minutes. Now, use "Quick Release" to release any pressure. Now remove the lid of the instant pot and wait for the steam to completely disperse.

Advice: If you want, then you are free to replace black pepper with white pepper.

Nutritional Information:

- **Servings Size: 2 cups**
- **Calories: 40**
- **Fiber: 1g**
- **Protein: 35**
- **Carb: 3g**
- **Fat: 0.5 g**
- **Sugar: 3g**
- **Cholesterol: 3 mg**
- **Sodium: 255 mg**

Recipe 7: Fresh vegetable and chicken salad steaks

- Cooking Time: 30 Minutes
- Cooking Level: Easy
- Vegetarian/Non-vegetarian: Non-Vegetarian
- Mode: Poultry

Ingredients:

- Minced chicken 1 cups
- Capsicum 1 cups chopped
- Onion one cups chopped
- Cabbage one cups chopped
- Apples one cups peeled and chopped
- White black pepper and salt as per your taste

Method:

Combine all ingredients in bowl. Add steaks to them. Marinate with all the spices. Add to the instant pot. Add water and then carefully cover with its lid and press "steam" button. Once you hear the final beep of instant pot, carefully release pressure with the help of instant release

Advice: If you want, replace water with stock to give it even better taste.

Nutritional Information:

- Servings Size: 3 cups
- Calories: 40
- Fiber: 1g
- Protein: 35
- Carb: 3g
- Fat: 0.5 g
- Sugar: 3g
- Cholesterol: 3 mg
- Sodium: 255 mg

Recipe 8: Low-Fat chicken Italia

- Cooking Time: 30 Minutes
- Cooking Level: Easy
- Vegetarian/Non-vegetarian: Non-Vegetarian
- Mode: Meat

Ingredients:

- Oregano one tsp.
- Salt as per your taste
- Boneless chicken one kg
- Oil 1 tsp.
- Pepper 1 tsp.
- Soy sauce one tsp.

Method:

Combine all ingredients in an instant pot. Cover its lid and select "Porridge" and cook on the manual setting. Once you get beep sound, turn the instant pot off and wait for ten minutes. Now, use "Quick

Release" to release any pressure. Now remove the lid of the instant pot and wait for the steam to completely disperse. Serve hot.

Advice: If you want, replace water with stock to give it even better taste.

Nutritional Information:

- **Servings Size: 4 cups**
- **Calories: 40**
- **Fiber: 1g**
- **Protein: 35**
- **Carb: 3g**
- **Fat: 0.5 g**
- **Sugar: 3g**
- **Cholesterol: 3 mg**
- **Sodium: 255 mg**

Recipe 9: Spicy chicken mince

- Cooking Time: 20 Minutes
- Cooking Level: Easy
- Vegetarian/Non-vegetarian: Non-Vegetarian
- Mode: Poultry

Ingredients:

- Chicken mince one kg
- White black pepper 1 tsp.
- Red black pepper flakes one a tsp.
- Onion chopped one cups
- Oil 1 tsp.

Method:

Add onion in instant pot followed by all other ingredients. Add water and then carefully cover with its lid and press "steam" button. Once you hear the final beep of instant pot, carefully release pressure with the help of instant release. Enjoy your meal.

Advice: If you want, replace water with stock to give it even better taste.

Nutritional Information:

- Servings Size: 2 cups
- Calories: 40
- Fiber: 1g
- Protein: 35
- Carb: 3g
- Fat: 0.5 g
- Sugar: 3g
- Cholesterol: 3 mg
- Sodium: 255 mg

Recipe 10: Tomato chicken with corn

- Cooking Time: 40 Minutes
- Cooking Level: Easy
- Vegetarian/Non-vegetarian: Non-Vegetarian
- Mode: Steam

Ingredients:

- Sweet corn one cups
- Chicken boiled one kg
- Soy sauce 1 tsp.
- Tomatoes fresh cubed one cups
- Black pepper 1 tsp.
- Salt as per your taste

Method:

Combine all ingredients in the instant pot. Cover its lid and select "Porridge" and cook on the manual setting. Once you get beep sound, turn the instant pot off and wait for ten minutes. Now, use "Quick Release" to release any pressure. Now remove the lid of the instant pot and wait for the steam to completely disperse. Serve hot.

Advice: If you want, replace water with stock to give it even better taste.

Nutritional Information:

- **Servings Size: 3 cups**
- **Calories: 40**
- **Fiber: 1g**
- **Protein: 35**
- **Carb: 3g**
- **Fat: 0.5 g**
- **Sugar: 3g**
- **Cholesterol: 3 mg**
- **Sodium: 255 mg**

Chapter 06: Instant pot dinner recipes

Recipe 1: Hot Beef steaks with mushrooms

- Cooking Time: 35 Minutes
- Cooking Level: Easy
- Vegetarian/Non-vegetarian: Non-Vegetarian
- Mode: Steam

Ingredients:

- Beef one cup boiled
- Mushrooms one cup
- Salt as per your taste
- Green onion one cup chopped
- Oil 2 tsp.
- Red chili 2 tsp.

Method:

Take an instant pot and add oil in it until it gets hot. Add onion and stir fry for about 2 minutes. Add rest of the ingredients.

Cover its lid and select "Meat" and cook on the manual setting. Once you get beep sound, turn the instant pot off and wait for ten minutes. Now remove the lid of the instant pot and wait for the steam to completely disperse.

Advice: If you want, replace water with stock to give it even better taste.

Nutritional Information:

- **Servings Size: 2 cup**
- **Calories: 45**
- **Fiber: 1g**
- **Protein: 45g**
- **Carb: 3g**
- **Fat: 0.5 g**
- **Sugar: 2g**
- **Cholesterol: 2 mg**
- **Sodium: 360 mg**

Recipe 2: Spicy beef steaks

- Cooking Time: 50 Minutes
- Cooking Level: Easy
- Vegetarian/Non-vegetarian: Non-Vegetarian
- Mode: Steam

Ingredients:

- Beef breast one kg
- All spices 2 tsp.
- Ginger paste 2 tsp.
- Garlic cloves 2 chopped

Method:

Add ginger paste and beef to an instant pot. Cover its lid and select "Meat" and cook on
the manual setting. Once you get beep sound, turn the instant pot off and wait for ten minutes. Now, use "Quick Release" to release any

pressure. Now remove the lid of the instant pot and wait for the steam to completely disperse. Mix well them well and cook until it gets hot.

Advice: If you want, replace water with stock to give it even better taste.

Nutritional Information:

- **Servings Size: 2 cup**
- **Calories: 45**
- **Fiber: 1 g**
- **Protein: 45g**
- **Carb: 3g**
- **Fat: 0.5 g**
- **Sugar: 2g**
- **Cholesterol: 2 mg**
- **Sodium: 360 mg**

Recipe 3: Crispy instant pot beef

- Cooking Time: 45 Minutes
- Cooking Level: Easy
- Vegetarian/Non-vegetarian: Non-Vegetarian
- Mode: Steam

Ingredients:

- Beef boneless (cut into strips) 2 kg
- Hot sauce one tsp.
- Oil 2 tsp.
- Onion chopped one cup
- Corn flour 2 tsp. salt as per your taste
- Whole wheat flour 2 tsp.

Method:

Mix well all the ingredients in a bowl except oil. Take an instant pot, add oil to it. Add the marinated mix well.

Cover its lid and select "Porridge" and cook on the manual setting. Once you get beep sound, turn the instant pot off and wait for ten minutes. Now, use "Quick Release" to release any pressure. Now remove the lid of the instant pot and wait for the steam to completely disperse.

Advice: If you want, replace water with stock to give it even better taste.

Nutritional Information:

- **Servings Size: 2 cup**
- **Calories: 45**
- **Fiber: 1 g**
- **Protein: 45g**
- **Carb: 3g**
- **Fat: 0.5 g**
- **Sugar: 2g**
- **Cholesterol: 2 mg**
- **Sodium: 360 mg**

Recipe 4: Beef fried rice with instant pot steaks

- Cooking Time: 25 Minutes
- Cooking Level: Easy
- Vegetarian/Non-vegetarian: Non-Vegetarian
- Mode: Steam

Ingredients:

- Boiled rice 2 cup
- Minced beef 2 cup
- Salt and black pepper as per your taste
- Oil 2 tsp.
- Green onion chopped 2 cup
- Capsicum chopped one cup
- Green peas 2 cup (boiled)

Method:

Add beef, salt and black pepper to an instant pot. Add all the vegetables as well.

Stir fry till becomes golden. Cover its lid and select "steam" and cook on the manual setting. Once you get beep sound, turn the instant pot off and wait for ten minutes. Now, use "Quick Release" to release any pressure. Now remove the lid of the instant pot and wait for the steam to completely disperse.

Advice: If you want, replace water with stock to give it even better taste.

Nutritional Information:

- **Servings Size: 2 cup**
- **Calories: 45**
- **Fiber: 1 g**
- **Protein: 45g**
- **Carb: 3g**
- **Fat: 0.5 g**
- **Sugar: 2g**
- **Cholesterol: 2 mg**
- **Sodium: 360 mg**

Recipe 5: Instant pot spicy Low-Fat chicken

- Cooking Time: 45 Minutes
- Cooking Level: Easy
- Vegetarian/Non-vegetarian: Non-Vegetarian
- Mode: Steam

Ingredients:

- Boneless chicken one kg
- Corn flour 2 tsp.
- Salt and black pepper as per your taste
- Oil 6 tsp.
- Green onion chopped one cup

Method:

Combine all ingredients in bowl and marinate for about an hour. Add oil to an instant pot and add the mixture into it. Cover its lid and select

"Meat/poultry" and cook on the manual setting. Once you get beep sound, turn the instant pot off and wait for ten minutes. Now, use "Quick Release" to release any pressure. Now remove the lid of the instant pot and wait for the steam to completely disperse.

Advice: If you want, replace water with stock to give it even better taste.

Nutritional Information:

- **Servings Size: 2 cup**
- **Calories: 45**
- **Fiber: 1 g**
- **Protein: 45g**
- **Carb: 3g**
- **Fat: 0.5 g**
- **Sugar: 2g**
- **Cholesterol: 2 mg**
- **Sodium: 360 mg**

Recipe 6: Instant pot beef fried peas

- Cooking Time: 30 Minutes
- Cooking Level: Easy
- Vegetarian/Non-vegetarian: Non-Vegetarian
- Mode: Steam

Ingredients:

- Beef boneless one kg
- Soy sauce 2 tsp.
- Salt as per your taste
- Peas one cup boiled
- Corn flour 2 tsp.
- Sesame seeds 2 tsp.

Method:

Add oil in an instant pot until it gets hot and add peas to it and stir fry them. Marinate beef in the ingredients mentioned above. Add beef to an instant pot in peas and stir fry Cover its lid and select "Porridge" and cook on the manual setting. Once you get beep sound, turn the instant pot off and wait for ten minutes. Now, use "Quick Release" to release any pressure. Now remove the lid of the instant pot and wait for the steam to completely disperse. Serve hot.

Advice: If you want, replace water with stock to give it even better taste.

Nutritional Information:

- **Servings Size: 2 cup**
- **Calories: 45**
- **Fiber: 1 g**
- **Protein: 45g**
- **Carb: 3g**
- **Fat: 0.5 g**
- **Sugar: 2g**
- **Cholesterol: 2 mg**
- **Sodium: 360 mg**

Recipe 7: Instant pot honey wings

- Cooking Time: 45 Minutes
- Cooking Level: Easy
- Vegetarian/Non-vegetarian: Non-Vegetarian
- Mode: Steam

Ingredients:

- Honey one cup
- Chicken wings 2 kg
- Oregano 2 tsp.
- Salt as per your taste
- Black pepper 2 tsp.
- Corn flour and rice flour one cup

Method:

Combine all the ingredients with chicken wings. Marinate for about 2o minutes. Cover its lid and select "Porridge" and cook on the manual setting. Once you get beep sound, turn the instant pot off and wait for ten minutes. Now, use "Quick Release" to release any pressure. Now remove the lid of the instant pot and wait for the steam to completely disperse.

Advice: If you want, replace water with stock to give it even better taste.

Nutritional Information:

- **Servings Size: 2 cup**
- **Calories: 45**
- **Fiber: 1g**
- **Protein: 45g**
- **Carb: 3g**
- **Fat: 0.5 g**
- **Sugar: 2g**
- **Cholesterol: 2 mg**
- **Sodium: 360 mg**

Recipe 8: Creamy chicken chunks

- Cooking Time: 45 Minutes
- Cooking Level: Easy
- Vegetarian/Non-vegetarian: Non-Vegetarian
- Mode: Steam

Ingredients:

- Chicken one kg
- Cream 450 grams
- Honey one tsp.
- Salt to taste
- Black pepper as per your taste

Method:

Add oil to an instant pot. Take a bowl and add all the ingredients in it. Marinate for about an hour. Add the marinated beef into oil in an instant pot.

Cover its lid and select "steam" and cook on the manual setting. Once you get beep sound, turn the instant pot off and wait for ten minutes. Now, use "Quick Release" to release any pressure. Now remove the lid of the instant pot and wait for the steam to completely disperse.

Advice: If you want, replace water with stock to give it even better taste.

Nutritional Information:

- **Servings Size: 2 cup**
- **Calories: 41**
- **Fiber: 1g**
- **Protein: 45g**
- **Carb: 3g**
- **Fat: 0.5 g**
- **Sugar: 2g**
- **Cholesterol: 2 mg**
- **Sodium: 243 mg**

Recipe 9: Orange and lemon lamb

- Cooking Time: 45 Minutes
- Cooking Level: Easy
- Vegetarian/Non-vegetarian: Non-Vegetarian
- Mode: Steam

Ingredients:

- Orange juice 2 cup
- Lemon juice 2 tsp.
- Boneless lamb one kg
- Barbeque sauce 2 tsp.
- Salt as per your taste
- Red black pepper flakes 2 tsp.

Method:

Take an instant pot and add all the ingredients in it. Cover its lid and select "steam" and cook on the manual setting. Once you get beep sound, turn the instant pot off and wait for ten minutes. Now, use

"Quick Release" to release any pressure. Now remove the lid of the instant pot and wait for the steam to completely settle.

Advice: If you want, replace water with stock to give it even better taste.

Nutritional Information:

- Servings Size: 2 cup
- Calories: 45
- Fiber: 1g
- Protein: 45g
- Carb: 3g
- Fat: 0.5 g
- Sugar: 2g
- Cholesterol: 2 mg
- Sodium: 360 mg

Recipe 10: Instant pot white beef

- Cooking Time: 45 Minutes
- Cooking Level: Easy
- Vegetarian/Non-vegetarian: Non-Vegetarian
- Mode: Steam

Ingredients:

- Garlic powder 2 tsp.
- All spices 2 tsp.
- Beef one kg
- Salt to taste
- Milk 2 tsp.
- Black pepper 2 tsp.
- Oil as per your taste
- Beef stock one cup

Method:

Add oil in an instant pot and switch on the stove. Add beef stock, milk and mayonnaise in an instant pot and mix well.

Add rest of the ingredients. Cover its lid and select "Porridge" and cook on the manual setting. Once you get beep sound, turn the instant pot off and wait for ten minutes. Now, use "Quick Release" to release any pressure. Now remove the lid of the instant pot and wait for the steam to completely disperse.

Advice: If you want, replace water with stock to give it even better taste.

Nutritional Information:

- **Servings Size: One bowl**
- **Calories: 45**
- **Fiber: 1g**
- **Protein: 45g**
- **Carb: 3g**
- **Fat: 0.5 g**
- **Sugar: 2g**
- **Cholesterol: 2 mg**
- **Sodium: 250 mg**

CHAPTER 07: Instant pot Recipes for Vegetarians (Beans and grains)

Recipe 1: Instant pot bean balls

- Cooking Time: 25 Minutes
- Cooking Level: Easy
- Vegetarian/Non-vegetarian: Vegetarian
- Mode: Steam

Ingredients:

- 4 ounces white onion, minced
- 2 tsp. butter
- 2 cold large egg
- Half tsp. sea salt
- Half tsp. freshly ground black pepper
- 3-4 tsp. herb seasonings of your choice
- 2 pound ground white beans

Directions

In a mixing dish, combine cheese and egg. Speed until smooth. Add the flavors, salt, and pepper and mix. Add beans and mix until all ingredients are mixed. Then, add all the ingredients to an instant pot. Then, carefully cover with its lid and press "Steam" button. Once you hear the final beep of instant pot, carefully release pressure with the help of instant release. Serve.

Advice: If you want, replace black pepper with white pepper to give it even better taste.

Nutritional Information:

- **Servings Size: 2 cup**
- **Calories: 25**
- **Fiber: 1g**
- **Protein: 25g**
- **Carb: 3g**
- **Fat: 0.5 mg**
- **Sugar: 2g**
- **Cholesterol: 0.2 mg**
- **Sodium: 360 mg**

Recipe 2: Instant pot Italian beans salad

- Cooking Time: 25 Minutes
- Cooking Level: Easy
- Vegetarian/Non-vegetarian: Vegetarian
- Mode: Steam

Ingredients:

- **4 ounces white onion, minced**
- **2 tsp. olive oil**
- **2 cold large egg**
- 2 tsp. Italian seasoning
- Half tsp. sea salt
- Half tsp. freshly ground black pepper
- 2 pound ground chickpeas

Directions

In a mixing dish, combine ricotta cheddar and egg. Rush until smooth. Add the flavors, salt, and pepper and mix. Mix well. Then, add all the ingredients to an instant pot. Then, carefully cover with its lid and press "Steam" button. Once you hear the final beep of instant pot, carefully release pressure with the help of instant release. Serve.

Advice: If you want, replace sea salt with black salt to give it even better taste.

Nutritional Information:

- Servings Size: 2 cup
- Calories: 25
- Fiber: 1g
- Protein: 25g
- Carb: 3g
- Fat: 0.8 mg
- Sugar: 2g
- Cholesterol: 0.2 mg
- Sodium: 360 mg

Recipe 3: Low-Fat beans and vegetable salsa

- Cooking Time: 35 Minutes
- Cooking Level: Easy
- Vegetarian/Non-vegetarian: Vegetarian
- Mode: Steam

Ingredients

- 2 tsp. of olive oil
- 2 large head organic cauliflower, trimmed and chopped into small pieces
- 2.5 ounces of white onion minced
- 2 tsp. butter
- Kidney beans (boiled) 1 cup
- Half cup of water
- 3 eggs
- 2 tsp. fennel seed
- 2 tsp. Italian seasoning

Directions

Add all the ingredients to an instant pot. Then, carefully cover with its lid and press "Steam" button. Once you hear the final beep of instant pot, carefully release pressure with the help of instant release. Serve.

Advice: If you want, replace Italian seasoning with Chinese seasoning to give it even better taste.

Nutritional Information:

- Servings Size: 2 cup
- Calories: 25
- Fiber: 1g
- Protein: 25g
- Carb: 3g
- Fat: 0.4 mg
- Sugar: 2g
- Cholesterol: 0.2 mg
- Sodium: 360 mg

Recipe 4: Instant pot Kidney beans

- Cooking Time: 25 Minutes
- Cooking Level: Easy
- Vegetarian/Non-vegetarian: Vegetarian
- Mode: Steam

Ingredients:

- 2 cloves garlic, minced
- 6 tsp. light olive oil
- 2 tsp. dried basil
- 2 tsp. salt
- 3 tsp. ground black pepper
- 2 tsp. lemon juice
- 1 tsp. fresh parsley, chopped
- 1 pound red or white kidney beans

Directions

In a medium glass dish, get ready marinade by mixing the garlic, light olive oil, basil, salt, pepper, lemon juice and parsley. Transfer all the ingredients to an instant pot. Then, carefully cover with its lid and press "Steam" button. Once you hear the final beep of instant pot, carefully release pressure with the help of instant release. Serve.

Advice: If you want, replace parsley with coriander to give it even better taste.

Nutritional Information:

- **Servings Size: 4 cups**
- **Calories: 25**
- **Fiber: 1g**
- **Protein: 25g**
- **Carb: 3g**
- **Fat: 0.7 mg**
- **Sugar: 2g**
- **Cholesterol: 0.2 mg**
- **Sodium: 360 mg**

Recipe 5: Instant pot egg whites and chickpeas salad

- Cooking Time: 45 Minutes
- Cooking Level: Easy
- Vegetarian/Non-vegetarian: Vegetarian
- Mode: Steam

Ingredients:

- 2 large eggs whites (Boiled and chopped)
- 2 tsp. of melted butter
- Half tsp. ground mustard
- 2/3 cup finely minced white onion
- 2 tsp. black pepper
- 2 tsp. salt

Directions

Then, add all the ingredients to an instant pot. Then, carefully cover with its lid and press "Steam" button. Once you hear the final beep of instant pot, carefully release pressure with the help of instant release. Serve.

Advice: If you want, replace minced onion with spring onion to give it even better taste.

Nutritional Information:

- **Servings Size: 4 cups**
- **Calories: 25**
- **Fiber: 1g**
- **Protein: 25g**
- **Carb: 3g**
- **Fat: 0.6 mg**
- **Sugar: 2g**
- **Cholesterol: 0.2 mg**
- **Sodium: 360 mg**

Recipe 6: Instant pot noodles with rice

- Cooking Time: 25 Minutes
- Cooking Level: Easy
- Vegetarian/Non-vegetarian: Vegetarian
- Mode: Porridge

Ingredients:

- Half cup fine vermicelli rice noodles
- Half cup beansprouts
- Zest and juice of 3 limes
- 3 tbsp. sesame seeds
- Half tsp oil

Directions:

Place the noodles and beansprouts in a heatproof bowl and cover with bubbling water. Then, add all the ingredients to an instant pot. Then, carefully cover with its lid and press "Steam" button. Once you hear the final beep of instant pot, carefully release pressure with the help of instant release. Serve.

Advice: If you want, replace lettuce with cabbage to give it even better taste.

Nutritional Information:

- **Servings Size: 4 cup**
- **Calories: 25**
- **Fiber: 1g**
- **Protein: 25g**
- **Carb: 3g**
- **Fat: 0.7 mg**
- **Sugar: 2g**
- **Cholesterol: 0.2 mg**
- **Sodium: 360 mg**

Recipe 7: Instant pot hot red kidney beans noodles

- Cooking Time: 40 Minutes
- Cooking Level: Easy
- Vegetarian/Non-vegetarian: Vegetarian
- Mode: Steam

Ingredients:

- Half cup Instant pot rice noodle
- 3 eggs
- Half thumb-size piece ginger
- Half cup red kidney beans
- Half tbsp. soy sauce
- ½ small bunch mint
- Zest and juice of half lime
- Half cup roasted peanuts, chopped

Directions:

Cook the noodles taking after the pack guidelines and put aside for some other time. Add the beans and ginger to a bowl, along with noodles, prawns and egg. Sprinkle in the soy sauce and then, add all the ingredients to an instant pot. Then, carefully cover with its lid and press "Steam" button. Once you hear the final beep of instant pot, carefully release pressure with the help of instant release. Serve.

Advice: If you want, replace lemon zest with orange zest to give it even better taste.

Nutritional Information:

- **Servings Size: 2 cup**
- **Calories: 25**
- **Fiber: 1g**
- **Protein: 25g**
- **Carb: 3g**
- **Fat: 0.9 mg**
- **Sugar: 2g**
- **Cholesterol: 0.2 mg**
- **Sodium: 360 mg**

Recipe 8: Instant pot fried rice with beans

- Cooking Time: 25 Minutes
- Cooking Level: Easy
- Vegetarian/Non-vegetarian: Vegetarian
- Mode: Steam

Ingredients:

- 3 tbsp. vegetable oil
- Half red onion, sliced
- 3 garlic clove, sliced
- Half cup kidney beans
- One cup cooked brown rice
- Quarter cup frozen pea
- Half tbsp. dark soy sauce
- Half tbsp. fish sauce
- Small bunch coriander, roughly chopped
- 4 large egg

Directions:

Add all the ingredients to an instant pot. Then, carefully cover with its lid and press "Steam" button. Once you hear the final beep of instant pot, carefully release pressure with the help of instant release. Serve.

Advice: If you want, replace dark soy sauce with usual soy sauce to give it even better taste.

Nutritional Information:

- Servings Size: 3 cup

- Calories: 25
- Fiber: 1g
- Protein: 25g
- Carb: 3g
- Fat: 0.2 mg
- Sugar: 2g
- Cholesterol: 0.2 mg
- Sodium: 360 mg

Recipe 9: Instant pot chickpeas with white sauce

- Cooking Time: 25 Minutes
- Cooking Level: Easy
- Vegetarian/Non-vegetarian: Vegetarian
- Mode: Porridge

Ingredients:

- 3 tbsp. vegetable oil
- 4 cloves garlic clove, pressed
- Half stalk lemon grass, crushed
- Half tbsp. oyster sauce
- Salt and pepper to taste
- 3 lbs. chickpeas

Directions:

Add the pounded garlic, ginger, and lemon grass and all other ingredients to an instant pot. Then, carefully cover with its lid and press "Steam"

button. Once you hear the final beep of instant pot, carefully release pressure with the help of instant release. Serve.

Advice: If you want, replace black pepper with white pepper to give it even better taste.

Nutritional Information:

- **Servings Size: 2 cup**
- **Calories: 25**
- **Fiber: 1g**
- **Protein: 25g**
- **Carb: 3g**
- **Fat: 0.5 mg**
- **Sugar: 2g**
- **Cholesterol: 0.2 mg**
- **Sodium: 360 mg**

Recipe 10: Instant pot Chickpeas

- Cooking Time: 25 Minutes
- Cooking Level: Easy
- Vegetarian/Non-vegetarian: Vegetarian
- Mode: Steam

Ingredients:

- **One cup brown rice noodle**
- **Half cup chickpeas**
- **Half tbsp. Instant pot red curry paste**
- **4 dried or fresh lime leaf**
- **Half tbsp. fish sauce**
- **Handful of coriander leaves**
-

Directions:

Then, add all the ingredients to an instant pot. Then, carefully cover with its lid and press "Steam" button. Once you hear the final beep of instant pot, carefully release pressure with the help of instant release. Serve.

*Advice: If you want, replace fish sauce
with soy sauce to give it even better taste.*

Nutritional Information:

Servings Size: 4 cups
Calories: 25
Fiber: 1g
Protein: 25g
Carb: 3g
Fat: 0.7 mg
Sugar: 2g
Cholesterol: 0.2 mg
Sodium: 360 mg

116

CHAPTER 08: Soup, Stews and Chilies in Instant pot

Recipe 1: Instant pot Sweet and sour tomato soup

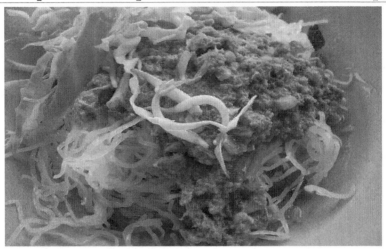

- Cooking Time: 25 Minutes
- Cooking Level: Easy
- Vegetarian/Non-vegetarian: Non-Vegetarian
- Mode: Steam

Ingredients:

- 4 cups chicken stock
- Half tbsp. tom yum paste
- Half clove garlic, finely chopped
- 4 stalks lemon grass, chopped
- 3 lime leaves
- 2 skinless, boneless chicken breast halves - shredded
- 3 oz. fresh mushrooms
- Half tbsp. fish sauce

Directions:

In the first step, take a large instant pot, heat the chicken stock to the point of boiling. Blend it in the tom yum paste and garlic and then add rest of the ingredients to the instant pot. Cover its lid and select "Porridge" and cook on the manual setting. Now remove the lid of the instant pot and wait for the steam to completely disperse.

Advice: If you want, replace lemon grass with coriander to give it even better taste.

Nutritional Information:

- Servings Size: 3 cups
- Calories: 25
- Fiber: 1g
- Protein: 25g
- Carb: 3g,
- Fat: 0.8 mg
- Sugar: 1g
- Cholesterol: 0.2 mg
- Sodium: 150 mg

Recipe 2: Green instant pot duck legs

- Cooking Time: 35 Minutes
- Cooking Level: Easy
- Vegetarian/Non-vegetarian: Non-Vegetarian
- Mode: Steam

Ingredients:

- Half tbsp. vegetable oil
- 4 duck legs
- Half small onion, chopped
- 4 cloves garlic, chopped
- 3 serrano peppers, seeded and chopped
- Half piece fresh ginger root, chopped
- Half bunch cilantro leaves

Directions:

Take an instant pot and add all the given ingredients one by one. Cover its lid and select "Steam" and cook on the manual setting. Once you get beep sound, turn the instant pot off and wait for ten minutes. Now, use

"Quick Release" to release any pressure. Now remove the lid of the instant pot and wait for the steam to completely disperse

Advice: If you want, replace cilantro leaves with oregano to give it even better taste.

Nutritional Information:

- Servings Size: 2 cup
- Calories: 25
- Fiber: 1g
- Protein: 25g
- Carb: 3g
- Fat: 0.5 mg
- Sugar: 1g
- Cholesterol: 0.2 mg
- Sodium: 250 mg

Recipe 3: Hot Lamb stews with mushrooms

- Cooking Time: 40 Minutes
- Cooking Level: Easy
- Vegetarian/Non-vegetarian: Non-Vegetarian
- Mode: Steam

Ingredients:

- Lamb one cup boiled
- Mushrooms one cup
- Salt as per your taste
- Green onion one cup chopped
- Oil 4 tsp.
- Red chili 1 tsp.

Method:

Take an instant pot and add all the given ingredients one by one. Cover its lid and select "Steam" and cook on the manual setting. Once you get beep sound, turn the instant pot off and wait for ten minutes. Now, use "Quick Release" to release any pressure. Now remove the lid of the instant pot and wait for the steam to completely disperse.

Advice: If you want, replace green onion with white onion to give it even better taste.

Nutritional Information:

- Servings Size: 2 cup
- Calories: 25
- Fiber: 1g
- Protein: 25g
- Carb: 3g
- Fat: 0.4 mg
- Sugar: 1g
- Cholesterol: 0.2 mg
- Sodium: 100 mg

Recipe 4: Spicy lamb stews

- Cooking Time: 25 Minutes
- Cooking Level: Easy
- Vegetarian/Non-vegetarian: Non-Vegetarian
- Mode: Steam

Ingredients:

- Oil 3 tsp.
- Lamb breast one kg
- All spices 1 tsp.
- Ginger paste 1 tsp.
- Garlic cloves 1 chopped

Method:

Add oil, ginger paste and lamb to an instant pot. Add rest of the ingredients which include spices and salt. Mix well them well and then cover its lid and select "Steam" and cook on the manual setting. Now, use "Quick Release" to release any pressure. Now remove the lid of the instant pot and wait for the steam to completely disperse.

Advice: If you want, replace water with stock to give it even better taste.

Nutritional Information:

- **Servings Size: 2 cups**
- **Calories: 25**
- **Fiber: 1g**
- **Protein: 25g**
- **Carb: 3g**
- **Fat: 0.1 mg**
- **Sugar: 1g**
- **Cholesterol: 0.2 mg**
- **Sodium: 100 mg**

Recipe 5: Crispy lamb golden stews

- Cooking Time: 25 Minutes
- Cooking Level: Easy
- Vegetarian/Non-vegetarian: Non-Vegetarian
- Mode: Steam

Ingredients:

- Lamb boneless (cut into strips) 1 kg
- Hot sauce 3 tsp.
- Oil 4 tsp.
- Onion chopped one cup
- Corn flour 4 tsp. salt as per your taste
- Whole wheat flour 1 tsp.

Method:

Mix well all the ingredients in a bowl except oil. Take an instant pot, add all the ingredients in it. Cover its lid and select "Steam" and cook on the manual setting. Now, use "Quick Release" to release any pressure. Now remove the lid of the instant pot and wait for the steam to completely disperse.

Advice: If you want, replace water with stock to give it even better taste.

Nutritional Information:

- **Servings Size: 4 cups**
- **Calories: 25**
- **Fiber: 1g**
- **Protein: 25g**
- **Carb: 3g**
- **Fat: 0.8 mg**
- **Sugar: 1g**
- **Cholesterol: 0.2 mg**
- **Sodium: 250 mg**

Recipe 6: Lamb fried rice with stews

- Cooking Time: 25 Minutes
- Cooking Level: Easy
- Vegetarian/Non-vegetarian: Non-Vegetarian
- Mode: Meat

Ingredients:

- Boiled rice 1 cup
- Minced lamb 1 cup
- Salt and black pepper as per your taste
- Oil 4 tsp.
- Green onion chopped 1 cup
- Capsicum chopped one cup
- Green peas half cup (boiled)

Method:

Add oil, lamb, salt and black pepper to instant pot. Add all the vegetables as well and then cover its lid and select "Meat" and cook on the manual setting. Once you get beep sound, turn the instant pot off and wait for ten minutes. Now, use "Quick Release" to release any pressure. Now remove the lid of the instant pot and wait for the steam to completely disperse.

Advice: If you want, replace capsicum with cabbage to give it even better taste.

Nutritional Information:

- **Servings Size: 2 cup**
- **Calories: 25**
- **Fiber: 1g**
- **Protein: 25g**
- **Carb: 3g**
- **Fat: 0.3 mg**
- **Sugar: 1g**
- **Cholesterol: 0.2 mg**
- **Sodium: 250 mg**

Recipe 7: Roasted spicy Low-Fat stews

- Cooking Time: 35 Minutes
- Cooking Level: Easy
- Vegetarian/Non-vegetarian: Non-Vegetarian
- Mode: Meat

Ingredients:

- Boneless lamb one kg
- Corn flour 4 tsp.
- Salt and black pepper as per your taste
- Oil 6 tsp.
- Green onion chopped one cup

Method:

Combine all ingredients in bowl and marinate for about an hour. Add oil to the instant pot and add the mixture into it. Cover its lid and select

"Meat" and cook on the manual setting. Once you get beep sound, turn the instant pot off and wait for ten minutes. Now, use "Quick Release" to release any pressure. Now remove the lid of the instant pot and wait for the steam to completely disperse.

Advice: If you want, replace green onion with white onion to give it even better taste.

Nutritional Information:

- **Servings Size: 2 cup**
- **Calories: 25**
- **Fiber: 1g**
- **Protein: 25g**
- **Carb: 3g**
- **Fat: 0.6 mg**
- **Sugar: 1g**
- **Cholesterol: 0.2 mg**
- **Sodium: 250 mg**

Recipe 8: Delicious coconut soup

- Cooking Time: 25 Minutes
- Cooking Level: Easy
- Vegetarian/Non-vegetarian: Non-Vegetarian
- Mode: Porridge

Ingredients:

- Half pound medium shrimp - peeled
- 3 (14 oz.) cans canned coconut milk
- 4 stalks lemon grass, bruised and chopped
- Half tbsp. green onion, thinly sliced
- Half tsp. dried red pepper flakes

Directions:

Pour the coconut milk and some water in a big instant pot, followed by addition of rest of the ingredients. Then, cover its lid and select "Porridge" and cook on the manual setting. Once you get beep sound, turn the instant pot off and wait for ten minutes. Now, use "Quick Release" to release any pressure. Now remove the lid of the instant pot and wait for the steam to completely disperse.

Advice: If you want, replace red pepper with green pepper to give it even better taste.

Nutritional Information:

- Servings Size: 2 cups
- Calories: 25
- Fiber: 1g
- Protein: 25g
- Carb: 3g
- Fat: 0.3 mg
- Sugar: 1g
- Cholesterol: 0.2 mg
- Sodium: 250 mg

Recipe 9: Instant pot red soup

- Cooking Time: 40 Minutes
- Cooking Level: Easy
- Vegetarian/Non-vegetarian: Non-Vegetarian
- Mode: Poultry

Ingredients:

- Half cup medium shrimp - peeled and deveined
- 15 mushrooms, halved
- Half (4.5 oz.) can mushrooms, milked
- 4 cups water
- Half tsp. white sugar

Directions:

Trim lemongrass and cut into matchstick size pieces. Add all the ingredients in an instant pot. Carefully cover with its lid and press "Poultry" button. Make sure to increase 10 minutes in default cooking time to cook the meat for almost 20 minutes. Once you hear the final beep of instant pot, carefully release pressure with the help of instant release. Serve.

Advice: If you want, replace white sugar with brown sugar to give it even better taste.

Nutritional Information:

- Servings Size: 2 cup
- Calories: 25
- Fiber: 1g
- Protein: 25g
- Carb: 3g
- Fat: 0.7 mg
- Sugar: 1g
- Cholesterol: 0.2 mg
- Sodium: 250 mg

Recipe 10: Special Instant pot green soup

- Cooking Time: 45 Minutes
- Cooking Level: Easy
- Vegetarian/Non-vegetarian: Non-Vegetarian
- Mode: Poultry

Ingredients:

- 3 tbsp. butter
- 3 tbsp. sliced green onion
- 4 cucumbers, peeled and chopped
- Quarter cup red vinegar
- Salt and black pepper to taste
- Half cup sour cream

Directions:

Add the green onions along with rest of the ingredients one by one in the instant pot. Carefully cover with its lid and press "Poultry" button. Once you hear the final beep of instant pot, carefully release pressure with the help of instant release. Serve.

Advice: If you want, replace red vinegar with white vinegar to give it even better taste.

Nutritional Information:

- Servings Size: 4 cups
- Calories: 25
- Fiber: 1g
- Protein: 25g
- Carb: 3g
- Fat: 0.6 mg
- Sugar: 1g
- Cholesterol: 0.2 mg
- Sodium: 250 mg

CHAPTER 09: Poultry and Seafood Instant Pot Recipes

Recipe 1: Prawn salsa

- Cooking Time: 25 Minutes
- Cooking Level: Easy
- Vegetarian/Non-vegetarian: Non-Vegetarian
- Mode: Meat

Ingredients:

- 3 bananas, peeled and thinly sliced
- 3 cucumbers
- 1/2 cup fresh mint leaves
- 1/2 cup fresh cilantro leaves
- 1/2 tsp. finely chopped
- Quarter cup lime juice
- 1/2 tbsp. fish sauce
- 1/2 tbsp. brown sugar
- 2 lbs. tiger prawns

Directions:

In a large dish, blend bananas, cucumbers, mint, cilantro, ginger, and red pepper to make salsa. Add all the ingredients to an instant pot. Then, carefully cover with its lid and press "meat" button. Make sure to increase 10 minutes in default cooking time to cook the meat for almost 20 minutes. Once you hear the final beep of instant pot, carefully release pressure with the help of instant release. Serve.

Advice: If you want, replace tiger prawns with simple prawns to give it a different taste.

Nutritional Information:

- **Servings Size: 2 cup**
- **Calories: 25**
- **Fiber: 1g**
- **Protein: 25g**
- **Carb: 3g**
- **Fat: 0.4 mg**
- **Sugar: 2g**
- **Cholesterol: 0.2 mg**
- **Sodium: 200 mg**

Recipe 2: Instant pot crabs

- **Cooking Time:** 25 Minutes
- **Cooking Level:** Easy
- **Vegetarian/Non-vegetarian:** Non-Vegetarian
- **Mode:** Meat

Ingredients:

- 1/2 pound crabmeat, flaked
- 1/2 tbsp. tamarind paste
- 3 pinches salt
- 1/2 egg whites, beaten

Directions:

In a medium dish, combine the crabmeat, tamarind paste, pepper and salt. Make sure to add all the ingredients to an instant pot. Then, carefully cover with its lid and press "meat" button. Make sure to increase 10 minutes in default cooking time to cook the meat for almost 20 minutes. Once you hear the final beep of instant pot, carefully release pressure with the help of instant release. Serve.

Advice: If you want, replace water with stock to give it even better taste.

Nutritional Information:

- Servings Size: 2 cup
- Calories: 25
- Fiber: 1g
- Protein: 25g
- Carb: 3g
- Fat: 0.8 mg
- Sugar: 2g
- Cholesterol: 0.2 mg
- Sodium: 200 mg

Recipe 3: Chicken green balls

- Cooking Time: 25 Minutes
- Cooking Level: Easy
- Vegetarian/Non-vegetarian: Non-Vegetarian
- Mode: Meat

Ingredients:

- 3 lbs. chopped chicken
- 1/2 tbsp. chopped coriander seed
- 1/2 cup chopped fresh cilantro
- Quarter cup sweet chili sauce
- 3 tbsp. fresh lemon juice

Directions:

In large dish, combine the chicken and bread morsels. Season with green onion, chopped coriander, cilantro, bean sauce and lemon juice, and blend well. Then add all the ingredients to an instant pot. Then, carefully cover with its lid and press "meat" button. Once you hear the final beep of instant pot, carefully release pressure with the help of instant release. Serve.

Advice: If you want, replace water with stock to give it even better taste.

Nutritional Information:

- **Servings Size: 2 cup**
- **Calories: 25**
- **Fiber: 1g**
- **Protein: 25g**
- **Carb: 3g**
- **Fat: 0.20 mg**
- **Sugar: 2g**
- **Cholesterol: 0.2 mg**
- **Sodium: 200 mg**

Recipe 4: Instant pot rolls with peanut butter sauce

- Cooking Time: 25 Minutes
- Cooking Level: Easy
- Vegetarian/Non-vegetarian: Non-Vegetarian
- Mode: Meat

Ingredients:

- 1/2 pound medium shrimp
- 1/2 (8 oz.) package rice noodles
- 15 round rice wrapper sheets
- 1/2 bunch fresh Instant pot basil leaves
- 1/2 cup chopped fresh cilantro
- 1/2 tbsp. water chopped roasted peanuts

Directions:

Add all the ingredients to an instant pot. Then, carefully cover with its lid and press "meat" button. Make sure to increase 10 minutes in default cooking time to cook the meat for almost 20 minutes. Once you hear the final beep of instant pot, carefully release pressure with the help of instant release. Serve.

Advice: If you want, replace water with stock to give it even better taste.

Nutritional Information:

- **Servings Size: 2 cup**
- **Calories: 25**
- **Fiber: 1g**
- **Protein: 25g**
- **Carb: 3g**
- **Fat: 0.5 mg**
- **Sugar: 2g**
- **Cholesterol: 0.2 mg**
- **Sodium: 200 mg**

Recipe 5: Chicken with mushrooms

- Cooking Time: 25 Minutes
- Cooking Level: Easy
- Vegetarian/Non-vegetarian: Non-Vegetarian
- Mode: Meat

Ingredients:

- One cup chopped fresh mushrooms
- Chicken (boneless) 1 kg
- 3 tbsp. basil pesto
- 3 tsp fish seasoning

Directions:

Blend together mushrooms, chicken, and seasonings over medium heat in an instant pot. Then, carefully cover with its lid and press "meat"

button. Once you hear the final beep of instant pot, carefully release pressure with the help of instant release. Serve.

Advice: If you want, replace water with stock to give it even better taste.

Nutritional Information:

- **Servings Size: 2 cup**
- **Calories: 25**
- **Fiber: 1g**
- **Protein: 25g**
- **Carb: 3g**
- **Fat: 0.6 mg**
- **Sugar: 2g**
- **Cholesterol: 0.2 mg**
- **Sodium: 200 mg**

Recipe 6: Instant pot Chicken

- Cooking Time: 25 Minutes
- Cooking Level: Easy
- Vegetarian/Non-vegetarian: Non-Vegetarian
- Mode: Meat

Ingredients:

- 5 lbs. fresh Chicken
- Quarter cup fresh lime juice
- 1/2 cup unsweetened coconut milk
- 1/2 tbsp. white sugar
- 3 cups chopped fresh cilantro

Directions:

In a big instant pot, combine the lime juice, coconut milk, wine, curry paste, garlic, fish sauce and sugar. Mix to break down sugar and curry paste. Then, carefully cover with its lid and press "meat" button. Once you hear the final beep of instant pot, carefully release pressure with the help of instant release. Serve.

Advice: If you want, replace water with stock to give it even better taste.

Nutritional Information:

- **Servings Size: 4 cups**
- **Calories: 25**
- **Fiber: 1g**
- **Protein: 25g**
- **Carb: 3g**
- **Fat: 0.3 mg**
- **Sugar: 2g**
- **Cholesterol: 0.2 mg**
- **Sodium: 200 mg**

Recipe 7: Crispy chicken

- Cooking Time: 25 Minutes
- Cooking Level: Easy
- Vegetarian/Non-vegetarian: Non-Vegetarian
- Mode: Meat

Ingredients:

- 4 cloves garlic, peeled
- 1/2 fresh jalapeno pepper, seeded
- 1/2 tsp. salt
- 1/2 tsp. chopped turmeric
- 3 tbsp. vegetable oil
- 1/2 cup coconut milk
- 4 tbsp. chopped fresh basil leaves

Directions:

Combine the garlic, ginger, jalapeno, salt and turmeric in the holder of a food processor or blender. Beat till a smooth paste is formed. Add

Chicken, and cook for a couple of minutes until pink, then add the tomatoes and coconut milk to the pot. Then, carefully cover with its lid and press "meat" button. Once you hear the final beep of instant pot, carefully release pressure with the help of instant release. Serve.

Advice: If you want, replace water with stock to give it even better taste.

Nutritional Information:

- Servings Size: 2 cup
- Calories: 25
- Fiber: 1g
- Protein: 25g
- Carb: 3g
- Fat: 0.7 mg
- Sugar: 2g
- Cholesterol: 0.2 mg
- Sodium: 200 mg

Recipe 8: Instant pot Tilapiya with sauce

- Cooking Time: 25 Minutes
- Cooking Level: Easy
- Vegetarian/Non-vegetarian: Non-Vegetarian
- Mode: Meat

Ingredients:

- 1/2 cup coconut milk
- 6 whole almonds
- 3 tbsp. chopped white onion
- Quarter tsp. salt
- Salt and pepper to taste
- 1/2 tsp. red pepper flakes

Directions:

In a food processor or blender, mix the coconut milk, almonds, onion, ginger, turmeric, lemon grass, and salt. Process until smooth. Add all the ingredients to an instant pot. Then, carefully cover with its lid and press "meat" button. Once you hear the final beep of instant pot, carefully release pressure with the help of instant release. Serve.

Advice: If you want, replace white onion with green onion to give it even better taste.

Nutritional Information:

- **Servings Size: 3 cups**
- **Calories: 25**
- **Fiber: 1g**
- **Protein: 25g**
- **Carb: 3g**
- **Fat: 0.5 mg**
- **Sugar: 2g**
- **Cholesterol: 0.2 mg**
- **Sodium: 200 mg**

Recipe 9: Chicken curry

- Cooking Time: 25 Minutes
- Cooking Level: Easy
- Vegetarian/Non-vegetarian: Non-Vegetarian
- Mode: Meat

Ingredients:

- 1/24 oz. canned coconut milk
- 3 tbsp. red Instant pot curry paste
- 1/2 tbsp. fish sauce
- 1/2 fresh red chili pepper, seeded and chopped
- Chicken, one pound

Directions:

In a dish, combine coconut milk, curry paste, fish sauce, and chopped pepper. Then transfer all the ingredients to an instant pot. Then, carefully cover with its lid and press "meat" button. Once you hear the final beep of instant pot, carefully release pressure with the help of instant release. Serve.

Advice: If you want, replace water with stock to give it even better taste.

Nutritional Information:

- Servings Size: 2 cup
- Calories: 25
- Fiber: 1g
- Protein: 25g
- Carb: 3g
- Fat: 0.6 mg
- Sugar: 2g
- Cholesterol: 0.2 mg
- Sodium: 200 mg

Recipe 10: Chicken instant pot noodles

- Cooking Time: 25 Minutes
- Cooking Level: Easy
- Vegetarian/Non-vegetarian: Non-Vegetarian
- Mode: Meat

Ingredients:

- 1/2 pound dried rice vermicelli
- 3 cups bean sprouts
- 4 tbsp. vegetable oil
- 1/2 tsp. chopped garlic
- 3 eggs, beaten
- 1/2 tbsp. chopped dry roasted peanuts
- 1/2 tsp. chili powder
- 3 wedges fresh lemon

Directions:

Place the noodles in a big bowl, and cover with water. Add the Chicken, Pour in the eggs, and blend for a moment. Then, add all the ingredients to an instant pot. Then, carefully cover with its lid and press "meat"

button. Once you hear the final beep of instant pot, carefully release pressure with the help of instant release. Serve.

Advice: If you want, replace water with stock to give it even better taste.

Nutritional Information:

- Servings Size: 2 cup
- Calories: 25
- Fiber: 1g
- Protein: 25g
- Carb: 3g
- Fat: 0.7 mg
- Sugar: 2g
- Cholesterol: 0.2 mg
- Sodium: 200 mg

CHAPTER 10: Beef, Lamb and Pork

Recipe 1: Fried beef with Snow Peas

- Cooking Time: 40 Minutes
- Cooking Level: Easy
- Vegetarian/Non-vegetarian: Non-Vegetarian
- Mode: Meat

Ingredients:

- 1 tablespoon ginger paste
- 4 medium raw scallions, chopped
- 1 tablespoon orange zest, crushed
- 1 cooking spray
- 2 garlic cloves, paste
- 8 oz. raw beef
- 3 cups snow peas
- 1/2 cup orange juice, fresh
- 2 cups raw bean sprouts
- 1.5 teaspoons honey

- 2 Tablespoons soy sauce, low salt
- 1.5 Tablespoons rice vinegar
- 1.5 teaspoon cornstarch
- 1 teaspoon sesame oil, toasted

Directions:

Add ginger, orange zest, scallions and garlic in the instant pot along with rest of the ingredients. Cover its lid and select "Meat" and cook on the manual setting. Once you get beep sound, turn the instant pot off and wait for ten minutes. Now, use "Quick Release" to release any pressure. Carefully remove the lid and wait for the steam to completely disperse.

Advice: You better use fresh sweet potatoes to avoid any lumps after mashing them.

Nutritional Value:

- **Servings Size: 1 cup**
- **Calories: 221**
- **Sodium: 113.5mg**
- **Total Fat: 1.5mg**
- **Cholesterol: 1.5mg**
- **Protein: 10g**

Recipe 2: Teriyaki Salad

- Cooking Time: 20 Minutes
- Cooking Level: Easy
- Vegetarian/Non-vegetarian: Non-Vegetarian
- Mode: Meat

Ingredients:

- Lamb steaks: 4
- Sesame oil: 2 teaspoons
- Oil: 2 teaspoons
- Salad greens (Asian): 200g

Dressing:

- Mirin Seasoning: 1/4 cup
- Rice-Wine Vinegar: 1/4 cup only
- Soy sauce: 1/4 cup only
- Castor sugar: 1/4 cup
- Pickled ginger to serve

Directions:

Take an instant pot and add all ingredients in it. Cover its lid and select "Meat" and cook on the manual setting. Once you get beep sound, turn the instant pot off and wait for ten minutes. Now, use "Quick Release" to release any pressure. Carefully remove the lid and wait for the steam to completely disperse.

Advice: You better use fresh sweet potatoes to avoid any lumps after mashing them.

Nutritional Value:

- Servings Size: 1 cup
- Calories: 221
- Sodium: 113.5mg
- Total Fat: 1.5mg
- Cholesterol: 1.5mg
- Protein: 10g

Recipe 3: Lamb with Noodles

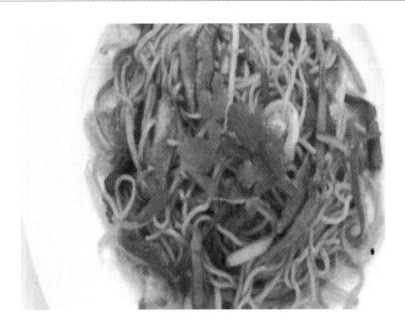

- Cooking Time: 20 Minutes
- Cooking Level: Easy
- Vegetarian/Non-vegetarian: Non-Vegetarian
- Mode: Meat

Ingredients:

- Lamb fillets: 2
- Soy sauce: 3 tablespoons
- Mirin: 3 tablespoons
- Spring Onions (chopped): 2 stalks
- Baby spinach: Large handful leaves
- Vegetable oil: 1 tablespoon
- Sesame seeds (toasted dry and hot frying instant pot): 2 teaspoon
- 1 Lime
- Sesame oil (toasted), for dressing: 2 teaspoon
- Soy sauce: 2 teaspoon

- Juice of 1 Lime

Directions:

Take one shallow bowl and mix soy sauce, lamb and mirin, mix them well and leave them for almost two hours. It will be good to keep it in the fridge for the whole night. Now, transfer these ingredients to an instant pot. Cover its lid and select "Meat" and cook on the manual setting. Once you get beep sound, turn the instant pot off and wait for ten minutes. Now, use "Quick Release" to release any pressure. Carefully remove the lid and wait for the steam to completely disperse.

Advice: Replace water with stock if desired.

Nutritional Information:

- **Servings Size: Half cup**
- **Calories: 20**
- **Fiber: 1g**
- **Protein: 20g**
- **Carb: 3g**
- **Fat: 3 g**
- **Sugar: 0g**
- **Cholesterol: 2 mg**
- **Sodium: 360 mg**

Recipe 4: Fried beef with Noodles

- Cooking Time: 50 Minutes
- Cooking Level: Easy
- Vegetarian/Non-vegetarian: Non-Vegetarian
- Mode: Meat

Ingredients:

- Chinese noodles: 360g
- Soy sauce: ¼ cup
- Mirin: ¼ cup
- Beef steak (large piece): 500g
- Olive oil: 1 tablespoon
- Baby spinach: 50g

Directions:

Noodles should be cooked as per the directions given on the pack and rinse the, under cold water. Mix mirin and soy in noodle. Then add rest of the ingredients and transfer them to the instant pot. Cover its lid and select "Meat" and cook on the manual setting. Once you get beep sound, turn the instant pot off and wait for ten minutes. Now, use "Quick Release" to release any pressure. Carefully remove the lid and wait for the steam to completely disperse.

Advice: Replace water with stock if desired.

Nutritional Information:

- **Servings Size: Half cup**
- **Calories: 20**
- **Fiber: 1g**
- **Protein: 20g**
- **Carb: 3g**
- **Fat: 3 g**
- **Sugar: 0g**
- **Cholesterol: 2 mg**
- **Sodium: 360 mg**

Recipe 5: Crispy Lamb steaks

- Cooking Time: 40 Minutes
- Cooking Level: Easy
- Vegetarian/Non-vegetarian: Non-Vegetarian
- Mode: Meat

Ingredients:

- Oil: 2 tablespoons
- Yellow egg noodles: 1 lb. (use cold water to rinse and drain)
- Minced garlic: 2 cloves
- Lamb steaks: 6 pieces (medium)
- Shredded Cabbage: 2 oz.
- Bean sprouts: 6 oz. (remove roots and rinse it with cold water)
- Salt: 1/4 teaspoon
- Chopped scallion for garnishing
- Tomato wedges for garnishing

Directions:

Add bean sprouts, cabbage and noodles in the pot along with rest of the ingredients. Then it is the time to mix noodles and all ingredients with a spatula for almost one minute to combine them thoroughly. Now cover the lid of instant pot and select "Meat" and cook on the manual setting. Once you get beep sound, turn the instant pot off and wait for ten minutes. Now, use "Quick Release" to release any pressure. Carefully remove the lid and wait for the steam to completely disperse.

Advice: Replace water with stock if desired.

Nutritional Information:

- **Servings Size: Half cup**
- **Calories: 20**
- **Fiber: 1g**
- **Protein: 20g**
- **Carb: 3g**
- **Fat: 3 g**
- **Sugar: 0g**
- **Cholesterol: 2 mg**
- **Sodium: 360 mg**

Recipe 6: Instant pot lamb Fried Rice

- Cooking Time: 30 Minutes
- Cooking Level: Easy
- Vegetarian/Non-vegetarian: Non-Vegetarian
- Mode: Meat

Ingredients:

- Lamb meat (green), roughly chopped: 200g
- Cooked Rice: 350 grams
- Lettuce leaves (thin slices): 4
- Chopped Garlic: 1 clove
- Red chili (chopped): 1/2
- Lamb Sauce (Fine): 1 ½ tablespoons
- Vegetable Oil: 2 tablespoons

Directions:

Add all the ingredients to an instant pot. Cover its lid and select "Meat" and cook on the manual setting. Once you get beep sound, turn the instant pot off and wait for ten minutes. Now, use "Quick Release" to release any pressure. Carefully remove the lid and wait for the steam to completely disperse.

Advice: Replace water with stock if desired.

Nutritional Information:

- **Servings Size: Half cup**
- **Calories: 20**
- **Fiber: 1g**
- **Protein: 20g**
- **Carb: 3g**
- **Fat: 3 g**
- **Sugar: 0g**
- **Cholesterol: 2 mg**
- **Sodium: 360 mg**

Recipe 7: Lamb with mixed vegetables

- Cooking Time: 45 Minutes
- Cooking Level: Easy
- Vegetarian/Non-vegetarian: Non-Vegetarian
- Mode: Meat

Ingredients:

- Carrot (you will cut strips): 1
- Lamb meat half kg
- Broccoli florets: 60g
- French beans: 60g
- Button mushrooms: 60g
- Diced Sweet Potato: 115g
- Olive Oil to Deep Fry
- Egg yolk: 1
- Ice-cold water: 450 ml
- Plain flour: 180g
- Soda (Bi-Carbonate): Pinch

Directions:

In the first step, you have to prepare a dipping sauce by letting the mirin boil in a cooking instant pot and keep on boiling until it reduced to half. Then add carrots and rest of the ingredients. It is time to add flakes and soy sauce and set the instant pot to "meat". Once you get beep sound, turn the instant pot off and wait for ten minutes. Now, use "Quick Release" to release any pressure. Carefully remove the lid and wait for the steam to completely disperse.

Advice: Replace water with stock if desired.

Nutritional Information:

- **Servings Size: Half cup**
- **Calories: 20**
- **Fiber: 1g**
- **Protein: 20g**
- **Carb: 3g**
- **Fat: 3 g**
- **Sugar: 0g**
- **Cholesterol: 2 mg**
- **Sodium: 360 mg**

Recipe 8: Instant pot beef with Eggplant

- Cooking Time: 30 Minutes
- Cooking Level: Easy
- Vegetarian/Non-vegetarian: Non-Vegetarian
- Mode: Meat

Ingredients:

- Eggplants (1.5cm round slices): 560g
- Spring onions, thin slices
- Olive oil 2 tablespoon
- Beef 1 pound
- Toasted sesame seeds, white, to serve
- Italian seasoning 1 tablespoon

Directions:

Take a mixing bowl to prepare a mixture of all wasabi-miso ingredients and whisk them well. Then transfer the ingredients to an instant pot.

Cover its lid and select "Meat" and cook on the manual setting. Once you get beep sound, turn the instant pot off and wait for ten minutes. Now, use "Quick Release" to release any pressure. Carefully remove the lid and wait for the steam to completely disperse.

Advice: Replace water with stock if desired.

Nutritional Information:

- **Servings Size: Half cup**
- **Calories: 20**
- **Fiber: 1g**
- **Protein: 20g**
- **Carb: 3g**
- **Fat: 3 g**
- **Sugar: 0g**
- **Cholesterol: 2 mg**
- **Sodium: 360 mg**

Recipe 9: Wasabi with Beef on White Rice

- Cooking Time: 45 Minutes
- Cooking Level: Easy
- Vegetarian/Non-vegetarian: Non-Vegetarian
- Mode: Meat

Ingredients:

- Sliced Beef steak: 500g
- Ground Black pepper
- Cooked Rice: 2 bowls

Sauce:

- Soy Sauce: 6 tablespoons
- Sugar: 1 ½ tablespoons
- Cooking sake: 2 tablespoons
- Apple sauce: 6 tablespoons

- Sesame oil: 1 tablespoon
- Minced Garlic: 1 clove
- Wasabi Paste: 1 tablespoon
- Sesame seeds: Roasted
- Thin slices of spring onions only to garnish

Directions:

To prepare sauce, you will let your cooking boil. Turn off heat and add other ingredients of sauce, whisk well and keep aside. Then add all the ingredients together. After that, cover its lid and select "Meat" and cook on the manual setting. Once you get beep sound, turn the instant pot off and wait for ten minutes. Now, use "Quick Release" to release any pressure. Carefully remove the lid and wait for the steam to completely disperse.

Advice: Replace water with stock if desired.

Nutritional Information:

- Servings Size: Half cup
- Calories: 20
- Fiber: 1g
- Protein: 20g
- Carb: 3g
- Fat: 3 g
- Sugar: 0g
- Cholesterol: 2 mg
- Sodium: 360 mg

Recipe 10: Ramen Noodles and lamb Steak

- Cooking Time: 40 Minutes
- Cooking Level: Easy
- Vegetarian/Non-vegetarian: Non-Vegetarian
- Mode: Meat

Ingredients:

- Ramen noodles: 270g
- Thin slices of lamb steak: 600g
- Fine slices of Red onion: 150g
- Fine slices of Red capsicum: 1
- Baby corn: 115g (lengthwise cuts in half)
- Trimmed snow peas: 150g
- Olive oil: 1 tablespoon
- Crushed garlic: 2 cloves
- Beef stock: 60ml
- Char-Sui sauce: ¼ cup

Directions:

Follow the packet instructions to cook noodles, drain them and refresh under running water. Drain them well and keep aside. Then add rest of the ingredients to an instant pot. Cover its lid and select "Meat" and cook on the manual setting. Once you get beep sound, turn the instant pot off and wait for ten minutes. Now, use "Quick Release" to release any pressure. Carefully remove the lid and wait for the steam to completely disperse. Serve hot.

Advice: Replace water with stock if desired.

Nutritional Information:

- **Servings Size: Half cup**
- **Calories: 20**
- **Fiber: 1g**
- **Protein: 20g**
- **Carb: 3g**
- **Fat: 3 g**
- **Sugar: 0g**
- **Cholesterol: 2 mg**
- **Sodium: 360 mg**

CHAPTER 11: Delicious Yogurt and Dessert in Instant Pot

Recipe 1: Low-Fat bread dessert

- Cooking Time: 15 Minutes
- Cooking Level: Easy
- Vegetarian/Non-vegetarian: Vegetarian
- Mode: Steam

Ingredients:

- 2 cup blanched almond flour
- Half tsp. baking powder
- Half tsp. Celtic sea salt
- 2 ounces cream cheese
- 2 tsp. butter
- 4 large eggs
- Half cup boiling water

Directions:

In a glass dish, mix the cream and margarine in a microwave. Add bubbling water at the same time into the dish. Then add all the above ingredients to your instant pot and stir all well with the help of wooden spoon. You may cook the above mixture for about 15 minutes on your instant pot. Carefully cover with its lid and press "steam" button. Once you hear the final beep of instant pot, carefully release pressure with the help of instant release. Take out the dessert and pour it into the bowl.

Advice: You better use baking soda to make the mixture fluffier.

Nutritional Value:

- **Servings Size: 2 cups**
- **Calories: 221**
- **Sodium: 113.5mg**
- **Total Fat: 1.5mg**
- **Cholesterol: 1.5mg**
- **Protein: 10g**

Recipe 2: Creamy Avocado with yoghurt

- Cooking Time: 15 Minutes
- Cooking Level: Easy
- Vegetarian/Non-vegetarian: Vegetarian
- Mode: Steam

Ingredients:

- 2 cup mayonnaise
- 2 tsp. lime juice
- 3 cloves garlic, minced
- 2 tablespoon yoghurt
- 2 tsp. salt
- 2 tsp. pepper
- 2 Haas avocados, seeded and mashed
- 2 cups heavy cream

Directions:

Mix all ingredients together which have been mentioned above. Add all of them to an instant pot. You may cook the above mixture for about 35 minutes on your instant pot. Carefully cover with its lid and press "steam" button. Once you hear the final beep of instant pot, carefully release pressure with the help of instant release. Take out the mixture and pour it into the bowl.

Advice: You better use baking soda to make the mixture fluffier.

Nutritional Value:

- **Servings Size: 2 cups**
- **Calories: 221**
- **Sodium: 113.5mg**
- **Total Fat: 1.5mg**
- **Cholesterol: 1.5mg**
- **Protein: 10g**

Recipe 3: Low-fat Yoghurt Sauce Recipe

- Cooking Time: 15 Minutes
- Cooking Level: Easy
- Vegetarian/Non-vegetarian: Vegetarian
- Mode: Steam

Ingredients:

- 3 tsp. butter
- 2 cups heavy cream
- 2 large egg yolks
- 2 cup yoghurt
- 2 tsp. granulated garlic
- 2 tsp. white pepper
- 2 tsp. herb of your choice

Directions:

Melt margarine in a medium instant pot over medium-high heat. Then whisk in the cream and egg yolk and cook for 5-6 minutes all the more, diminishing the heat to medium low. Then mix all ingredients together which have been mentioned above. Add all of them to an instant pot.

You may cook the above mixture for about 45 minutes on your instant pot. Carefully cover with its lid and press "porridge" button. Once you hear the final beep of instant pot, carefully release pressure with the help of instant release. Take out the mixture and pour it into the bowl.

Advice: You better use baking soda to make the mixture fluffier.

Nutritional Value:

- **Servings Size: 2 cups**
- **Calories: 221**
- **Sodium: 113.5mg**
- **Total Fat: 1.5mg**
- **Cholesterol: 1.5mg**
- **Protein: 10g**

Recipe 4: Cream Sparkler

- Cooking Time: 15 Minutes
- Cooking Level: Easy
- Vegetarian/Non-vegetarian: Vegetarian
- Mode: Steam

Ingredients:

- 4 ounces heavy cream
- 2 tsp. Sugar Free Raspberry Syrup
- Sparkling flavored water, such as La Croix berry flavor

Directions:

Put cream and raspberry syrup in an instant pot. Then mix rest of the ingredients together which have been mentioned above. Add all of them to an instant pot. You may cook the above mixture for about 45 minutes on your instant pot. Carefully cover with its lid and press "porridge" button. Once you hear the final beep of instant pot, carefully release pressure with the help of instant release. Take out the mixture and pour it into the bowl.

Advice: You better use baking soda to make the mixture fluffier.

Nutritional Value:

- **Servings Size: 2 cups**
- **Calories: 221**
- **Sodium: 113.5mg**
- **Total Fat: 1.5mg**
- **Cholesterol: 1.5mg**
- **Protein: 10g**

Recipe 5: Instant pot Chocolate Raspberry dessert

- Cooking Time: 15 Minutes
- Cooking Level: Easy
- Vegetarian/Non-vegetarian: Vegetarian
- Mode: Steam

Ingredients:

- 6 ounces almond milk
- 2 ounces heavy cream
- 4 scoops Chocolate Whey Isolate powder
- 2 tsp. Sugar Free Raspberry Syrup
- Half cup crushed ice

Directions:

Put all ingredients in mixer and mix until smooth. Then add all of them to an instant pot. You may cook the above mixture for about 15 minutes on your instant pot. Carefully cover with its lid and press "porridge" button. Once you hear the final beep of instant pot, carefully release pressure with the help of instant release. Take out the mixture and pour it into the bowl. Serve cold after putting it in refrigerator for about 2 hours.

Advice: You better use baking soda to make the mixture fluffier.

Nutritional Value:

- Servings Size: 2 cups
- Calories: 221
- Sodium: 113.5mg
- Total Fat: 1.5mg
- Cholesterol: 1.5mg
- Protein: 10g

Recipe 6: White Chocolate Almond Protein dessert

- Cooking Time: 15 Minutes
- Cooking Level: Easy
- Vegetarian/Non-vegetarian: Vegetarian
- Mode: Steam

Ingredients:

- 15 ounces unsweetened almond milk
- 6 ounces heavy cream
- 4 scoops Vanilla Whey Powder
- 2 tsp. Chocolate syrup
- 2 cups crushed ice

Directions:

Put all ingredients in mixer and mix until smooth. Then add all of them to an instant pot. You may cook the above mixture for about 15 minutes on your instant pot. Carefully cover with its lid and press "porridge" button. Once you hear the final beep of instant pot, carefully release pressure with the help of instant release. Take out the mixture and pour it into the bowl. Serve cold after putting it in refrigerator for about 2 hours.

Advice: You better use baking soda to make the mixture fluffier.

Nutritional Value:

- **Servings Size: 2 cups**
- **Calories: 221**
- **Sodium: 113.5mg**
- **Total Fat: 1.5mg**
- **Cholesterol: 1.5mg**
- **Protein: 10g**

Recipe 7: Instant pot Coconut Protein dessert

-
- Cooking Time: 15 Minutes
- Cooking Level: Easy
- Vegetarian/Non-vegetarian: Vegetarian
- Mode: Steam

Ingredients:

- 15 ounces unsweetened almond milk
- 6 ounces heavy cream
- 4 scoops Whey Powder
- 2 tsp. Coconut Syrup
- Half cup crushed ice

Directions:

Put all ingredients in mixer and mix until smooth. Then add all of them to an instant pot. You may cook the above mixture for about 15 minutes on your instant pot. Carefully cover with its lid and press "porridge" button. Once you hear the final beep of instant pot, carefully release pressure with the help of instant release. Take out the mixture and pour it into the bowl. Serve cold after putting it in refrigerator for about 2 hours.

Advice: You better use baking soda to make the mixture fluffier.

Nutritional Value:

- Servings Size: 2 cups
- Calories: 221
- Sodium: 113.5mg
- Total Fat: 1.5mg
- Cholesterol: 1.5mg
- Protein: 10g

Recipe 8: Creamy Chocolate dessert

- Cooking Time: 15 Minutes
- Cooking Level: Easy
- Vegetarian/Non-vegetarian: Vegetarian
- Mode: Steam

Ingredients:

- 6 ounces unsweetened almond milk
- Quarter packet artificial sweetener
- 2 ounces heavy cream
- Half scoop cocoa powder
- Half cup crushed ice

Directions:

Put all ingredients in mixer. Mix them well. Then add all of them to an instant pot. You may cook the above mixture for about 10 minutes on your instant pot. Carefully cover with its lid and press "porridge" button. Once you hear the final beep of instant pot, carefully release pressure with the help of instant release. Take out the mixture and pour it into the bowl. Serve cold after putting it in refrigerator for about 5 hours.

Advice: You better use baking soda to make the mixture fluffier.

Nutritional Value

- **Servings Size: 2 cups**
- **Calories: 221**
- **Sodium: 113.5mg**
- **Total Fat: 1.5mg**
- **Cholesterol: 1.5mg**
- **Protein: 10g**

Recipe 9: Instant pot mango and rice pudding

- Cooking Time: 15 Minutes
- Cooking Level: Easy
- Vegetarian/Non-vegetarian: Vegetarian
- Mode: Steam

Ingredients:

- Half Quarter cups raw sticky rice
- Half cup very thick coconut milk for mixing with rice
- Quarter cup sugar
- Half cup very thick coconut milk for topping the rice
- A pinch of salt for the topping
- Half tbsp.. salt for mixing with rice
- Quarter tsp rice flour
- 6 medium mangoes — peeled and sliced

Directions:

Wash the sticky rice well. Add enough water to the rice so until the water is around Quarter over the rice surface. Then add rest of the ingredients. Carefully cover with its lid and press "porridge" button. Once you hear the final beep of instant pot, carefully release pressure with the help of instant release. Take out the mixture and pour it into the bowl. Serve cold after putting it in refrigerator for about 2 hours.

Advice: You better use baking soda to make the mixture fluffier.

Nutritional Value:

- **Servings Size: 2 cups**
- **Calories: 221**
- **Sodium: 113.5mg**
- **Total Fat: 1.5mg**
- **Cholesterol: 1.5mg**
- **Protein: 10g**

Recipe 10: Instant pot coconut cream

- Cooking Time: 15 Minutes
- Cooking Level: Easy
- Vegetarian/Non-vegetarian: Vegetarian
- Mode: Steam

Ingredients

- 6 bananas
- 15 oz. coconut milk
- 3 tbsp. granulated sugar
- Half tsp salt

Directions:

Peel the bananas and cut into 3 inches pieces. In an instant pot, add the coconut milk with the sugar and salt, and cook delicately until the sugar broke down. Add the banana pieces and then carefully cover with its lid and press "porridge" button. Once you hear the final beep of instant pot, carefully release pressure with the help of instant release. Take out the mixture and pour it into the bowl. Serve cold after putting it in refrigerator for about 2 hours.

Advice: You better use baking soda to make the mixture fluffier.

Nutritional Value:

- **Servings Size: 2 cups**
- **Calories: 221**
- **Sodium: 113.5mg**
- **Total Fat: 1.5mg**
- **Cholesterol: 1.5mg**
- **Protein: 10g**

CHAPTER 12: Grains, Beans, Lentils and Rice Recipes

Recipe 1: Instant pot Chickpeas with rice

- Cooking Time: 25 Minutes
- Cooking Level: Easy
- Vegetarian/Non-vegetarian: Vegetarian
- Mode: Steam

Ingredients

- Chickpeas: 300g
- Soy sauce: 3 tablespoons
- Mirin: 3 tablespoons
- Fine slices of Ginger: 10 grams
- Fine slices of Spring onion: 1
- Rice: 1 cup

Directions:

Dip the chickpeas into corn flour. Put all the other ingredients in mixer as well and mix until smooth. Then add all of them to an instant pot.

You may cook the above mixture for about 15 minutes on your instant pot. Carefully cover with its lid and press "steam" button. Once you hear the final beep of instant pot, carefully release pressure with the help of instant release. Take out the mixture and pour it into the bowl.

Advice: If you want, replace water with stock to give it even better taste.

Nutritional Information:

- **Servings Size: 2 cups**
- **Calories: 40**
- **Fiber: 1g**
- **Protein: 35**
- **Carb: 3g**
- **Fat: 0.5mg**
- **Sugar: 3g**
- **Cholesterol: 0.3mg**
- **Sodium: 255 mg**

Recipe 2: Chickpeas and Mushroom Salad

- Cooking Time: 25 Minutes
- Cooking Level: Easy
- Vegetarian/Non-vegetarian: Vegetarian
- Mode: Steam

Ingredients:

- Chopped Fresh chives: ½ bunch
- Slices of Spring onions: 2 stalks
- Olive oil: 1 to 2 tablespoons
- Sliced brown mushrooms: 6
- Black pepper and Sea salt as per taste
- Chickpeas: Half cup
- Toasted Sesame seeds: 3 tablespoons
- Soy sauce: 4 tablespoons
- Olive oil (extra virgin): 4 tablespoons
- Raw sugar: 2 teaspoons

Directions:

Follow instructions given on the packet to cook noodles, drain and refresh under running water, once again drain well and keep aside. Use a mixing bowl to prepare dressing and whisk soy sauce, sesame seeds, vinegar, olive oil and sugar. Keep it aside. Take a large bowl and add chives along with spring onions. Then add all of them to an instant pot.

You may cook the above mixture for about 40 minutes on your instant pot. Carefully cover with its lid and press "steam" button. Once you hear the final beep of instant pot, carefully release pressure with the help of instant release. Take out the mixture and pour it into the bowl.

Advice: If you want, replace water with stock to give it even better taste.

Nutritional Information:

- **Servings Size: 2 cups**
- **Calories: 40**
- **Fiber: 1g**
- **Protein: 35**
- **Carb: 3g**
- **Fat: 0.5mg**
- **Sugar: 3g**
- **Cholesterol: 0.3mg**
- **Sodium: 255 mg**

Recipe 3: Red lentils salsa

- Cooking Time: 25 Minutes
- Cooking Level: Easy
- Vegetarian/Non-vegetarian: Vegetarian
- Mode: Steam

Ingredients:

- Soy sauce: 3/4 cup (you can mix water and tamari in equal proportions to use as alternative)
- Red lentils: 3/4 cup
- Mirin: 3/4 cup
- Sugar: 4 Tablespoons
- Finely grated ginger: 1-inch piece
- Sesame seeds: 2 to 3 tablespoons

Directions:

Take a cooking pot to mix sugar, grated ginger, mirin, sake, and soy sauce. Put all ingredients in mixer and mix until smooth. Then add all of them to an instant pot. You may cook the above mixture for about 15 minutes on your instant pot. Carefully cover with its lid and press "steam" button. Once you hear the final beep of instant pot, carefully release pressure with the help of instant release. Take out the mixture and pour it into the bowl.

Advice: If you want, replace water with stock to give it even better taste.

Nutritional Information:

- Servings Size: 2 cups
- Calories: 40
- Fiber: 1g
- Protein: 35
- Carb: 3g
- Fat: 0.5mg
- Sugar: 3g
- Cholesterol: 0.3mg
- Sodium: 255 mg

Recipe 4: Green lentils and eel salad

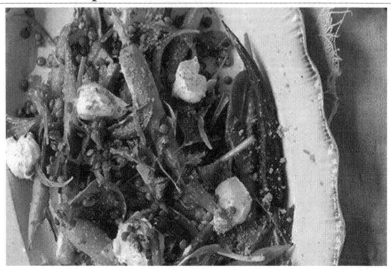

- Cooking Time: 25 Minutes
- Cooking Level: Easy
- Vegetarian/Non-vegetarian: Non-Vegetarian
- Mode: Steam

Ingredients:

- Eel steak: 1 lb
- Sake: 3 tablespoons
- Mirin: 2 tablespoons
- Green lentils: 1 cup
- Sugar: 4 teaspoons
- Fish stock: 1/2 cup
- Soy sauce: 2 tablespoons

Directions:

Take a pot and put soy sauce, sake, fish stock, green lentils and sugar. Then transfer all of them to an instant pot. You may cook the above mixture for about 15 minutes on your instant pot. Carefully cover with its lid and press "steam" button. Once you hear the final beep of instant pot, carefully release pressure with the help of instant release. Take out the mixture and pour it into the bowl.

Advice: If you want, replace water with stock to give it even better taste.

Nutritional Information:

- **Servings Size: 2 cups**
- **Calories: 40**
- **Fiber: 1g**
- **Protein: 35**
- **Carb: 3g**
- **Fat: 0.5mg**
- **Sugar: 3g**
- **Cholesterol: 0.3mg**
- **Sodium: 255 mg**

Recipe 5: Lentils and Eggs rice

- Cooking Time: 25 Minutes
- Cooking Level: Easy
- Vegetarian/Non-vegetarian: Vegetarian
- Mode: Steam

Ingredients:

- Garlic: 1 clove
- Eggs: 4
- Ginger: 2 slices
- Rice: 1 cup

Spices:

- Sake: ¼ cup
- Soy sauce: ¼ cup
- Sesame oil: ½ teaspoon

Directions:

Take an instant pot and boil mirin, sake, ½ cup water and soy sauce. Then mix garlic, sesame oil and ginger. Then add all of them to an instant pot. You may cook the above mixture for about 15 minutes on your instant pot. Carefully cover with its lid and press "steam" button. Once you hear the final beep of instant pot, carefully release pressure with the help of instant release. Take out the mixture and pour it into the bowl.

Advice: If you want, replace water with stock to give it even better taste.

Nutritional Information:

- **Servings Size: 2 cups**
- **Calories: 40**
- **Fiber: 1g**
- **Protein: 35**
- **Carb: 3g**
- **Fat: 0.5mg**
- **Sugar: 3g**
- **Cholesterol: 0.3mg**
- **Sodium: 255 mg**

Recipe 6: Egg fried rice Rolls

- Cooking Time: 25 Minutes
- Cooking Level: Easy
- Vegetarian/Non-vegetarian: Vegetarian
- Mode: Steam

Ingredients:

- Rice: 1 cup
- Water: 500ml
- Italian seasoning: 1 teaspoon
- Ginger: 2 tablespoon
- Egg whites: 4

Directions:

In the first step, you have to cook rice in 500ml water, pour rice, turn on heat and let the water boil in an instant pot. You should stir occasionally and cover the rice for 10 to 14 minutes by lowering heat. Remove your rice from heat, but let them cover for 5 to 10 minutes. Then add rest of the ingredients to the pot along with rice. You may cook the above mixture for about 15 minutes on your instant pot. Carefully cover with its lid and press "steam" button. Once you hear the final beep of instant pot, carefully release pressure with the help of instant release. Take out the mixture and pour it into the bowl.

Advice: If you want, replace water with stock to give it even better taste.

Nutritional Information:

- **Servings Size: 2 cups**
- **Calories: 40**
- **Fiber: 1g**
- **Protein: 35**
- **Carb: 3g**
- **Fat: 0.5mg**
- **Sugar: 3g**
- **Cholesterol: 0.3mg**
- **Sodium: 255 mg**

Recipe 7: Instant pot spicy rice noodles

- Cooking Time: 25 Minutes
- Cooking Level: Easy
- Vegetarian/Non-vegetarian: Vegetarian
- Mode: Steam

Ingredients:

- Half cup fine vermicelli rice noodles
- Half cup beansprouts
- Zest and juice of 3 limes
- 3 tbsp. sesame seeds
- Half tsp oil

Directions:

Place the noodles and beansprouts in a heatproof bowl. Then add all of the ingredients to an instant pot. You may cook the above mixture for about 15 minutes on your instant pot. Carefully cover with its lid and press "steam" button. Once you hear the final beep of instant pot, carefully release pressure with the help of instant release. Take out the mixture and pour it into the bowl.

Advice: If you want, replace water with stock to give it even better taste.

Nutritional Information:

- Servings Size: 2 cups
- Calories: 40
- Fiber: 1g
- Protein: 35
- Carb: 3g
- Fat: 0.5mg
- Sugar: 3g
- Cholesterol: 0.3mg
- Sodium: 255 mg

Recipe 8: Instant pot hot red lentils noodles

- Cooking Time: 25 Minutes
- Cooking Level: Easy
- Vegetarian/Non-vegetarian: Vegetarian
- Mode: Steam

Ingredients:

- Half cup Instant pot rice noodle
- Half tbsp. sesame oil
- 3 eggs
- Half thumb-size piece ginger
- Half cup cooked red lentils
- Half tbsp. soy sauce
- ½ small bunch mint
- Zest and juice Half lime
- Half cup roasted peanuts, chopped

Directions:

Cook the noodles taking after the pack guidelines. Then add all the ingredients in them. Then add all of them to an instant pot. You may cook the above mixture for about 15 minutes on your instant pot. Carefully cover with its lid and press "steam" button. Once you hear the final beep of instant pot, carefully release pressure with the help of instant release. Take out the mixture and pour it into the bowl.

Advice: If you want, replace water with stock to give it even better taste.

Nutritional Information:

- **Servings Size: 2 cups**
- **Calories: 40**
- **Fiber: 1g**
- **Protein: 35**
- **Carb: 3g**
- **Fat: 0.5mg**
- **Sugar: 3g**
- **Cholesterol: 0.3mg**
- **Sodium: 255 mg**

Recipe 9: Instant pot fried rice with peas and red lentils

- Cooking Time: 25 Minutes
- Cooking Level: Easy
- Vegetarian/Non-vegetarian: Non-Vegetarian
- Mode: Steam

Ingredients:

- 3 tbsp. vegetable oil
- Half red onion, sliced
- 3 garlic clove, sliced
- Half red chili, sliced
- Half cup raw red lentils
- One cup cooked brown rice
- Quarter cup frozen pea
- Half tbsp. dark soy sauce
- Half tbsp. fish sauce
- Small bunch coriander, roughly chopped
- 4 large egg

Directions:

Add all of the ingredients to an instant pot. You may cook the above mixture for about 15 minutes on your instant pot. Carefully cover with its lid and press "steam" button. Once you hear the final beep of instant pot, carefully release pressure with the help of instant release. Take out the mixture and pour it into the bowl.

Advice: If you want, replace water with stock to give it even better taste.

Nutritional Information:

- Servings Size: 2 cups
- Calories: 40
- Fiber: 1g
- Protein: 35
- Carb: 3g
- Fat: 0.5mg
- Sugar: 3g
- Cholesterol: 0.3mg
- Sodium: 255 mg

Recipe 10: Instant pot fish rice with chickpeas

- Cooking Time: 25 Minutes
- Cooking Level: Easy
- Vegetarian/Non-vegetarian: Non-Vegetarian
- Mode: Steam

Ingredients:

- One cup chickpeas (boiled)
- Half cup chicken or fish stock
- Half tbsp. red curry paste
- 4 dried or fresh lime leaf
- Half tbsp. fish sauce
- Handful coriander leaves

Directions:

Add all of the ingredients to an instant pot. You may cook the above mixture for about 15 minutes on your instant pot. Carefully cover with its lid and press "steam" button. Once you hear the final beep of instant pot, carefully release pressure with the help of instant release. Take out the mixture and pour it into the bowl.

Advice: If you want, replace water with stock to give it even better taste.

Nutritional Information:

- Servings Size: 2 cups
- Calories: 40
- Fiber: 1g
- Protein: 35
- Carb: 3g
- Fat: 0.5mg
- Sugar: 3g
- Cholesterol: 0.3mg
- Sodium: 255 mg

Conclusion

I hope this book will help you out in making the Low-Fat instant pot recipes in an easy way. As a health food nut, a strict Low-Fat diet plan, constraining fats and cholesterol, by cooking in electric instant pot will bring about a lot of advantages for you. Analysts keep on contemplating the impacts, both positive and negative of Low-Fat instant pot recipes. The primary advantage of cooking in an instant pot is that, you save your time and also, a Low-Fat recipe can be made very easily using it.

In this book, I have added every type of recipe which you will like to have. Baby food, food for adults, breakfast, lunch and dinner recipes, meat recipes which include lamb, beef and chicken and instant pot dessert recipes have also been added. The book has got a variety of recipes with all the nutritional information, serving size and cooking time etc. I hope you have enjoyed this book and you will try the recipes as well.

Your Free Gift

I wanted to show my appreciation that you support my work so I've put together a free gift for you.

Get Your Free Gift Here:
http://www.cbookreadzone.com

Just visit the link above to download it now.

I know you will love this gift.

Thanks!

John Raney

Copyright 2014 by John Raney - All rights reserved.

35961962R00134

Made in the USA
Middletown, DE
21 October 2016